The Great British
Butterfly Safari

The Great British
Butterfly Safari

Robin Page

Illustrations by John Paley
Foreword by Willie Poole MBE

BIRD'S FARM BOOKS

By the Same Author

The Benefits Racket
Down Among the Dossers
The Decline of an English Village
The Hunter and the Hunted
Weather-forecasting the Country Way
Cures and Remedies the Country Way
Animal Cures the Country Way
Weeds the Country Way
The Journal of a Country Parish
Journeys into Britain
The Country Way of Love
The Wildlife of the Royal Estates
A Fox's Tale
The Fox and the Orchid
Dust in a Dark Continent (Africa)
Gardening the Country Way
A Peasant's Diary
Gone to the Dogs
Vocal Yokel
Carry on Farming
The Hunting Gene
One Man Went to Mow

Children's Books

How the Fox got its Pointed Nose
How the Heron got Long Legs
Why the Rabbit Stamps its Foot
How the Hedgehog got its Prickles
Why the Reindeer has a Velvet Nose

Published by Bird's Farm Books, Barton, Cambridgeshire CB3 7AG
www.crtbarton.com
Distributed by Merlin Unwin Books, 7 Corve Street, Ludlow, Shropshire

Text © Robin Page 2003
Illustrations © John Paley 2003

ISBN 0-905232-22-4

Designed by Jim Reader
Design and production in association with Book Production Consultants plc,
25–27 High Street, Chesterton, Cambridge CB4 1ND
www.bpccam.co.uk

Printed and bound in Great Britain by the Cromwell Press, Trowbridge, Wilts.

CONTENTS

FOREWORD – Willie Poole MBE

THE GREAT BRITISH BUTTERFLY SAFARI was a splendid adventure designed to commemorate a good man – Gordon Beningfield – artist, conservationist and fighter for the countryside. The aim was to raise money for the Gordon Beningfield Memorial Appeal by trying to see every species of British butterfly on the wing in a single summer – for sponsorship. Robin Page had a simple idea – well any idea from him would be simple wouldn't it? But I have to admit, reluctantly, that it was also a good idea.

However – it got better by accident. When tired, old, bumpkinesque Page was on safari in Africa, he met vivacious young city-sophisticate Sarah Golding from the swinging side of London – young enough to be his grown-up daughter, but a lot better looking. Page knows nothing about the city – Sarah knew little about the country; she even had a shock when she was told that certain large pink things with four legs in a field were known as 'pigs'.

With bizarre bad taste she decided to continue her Africa safari on into the Great British Butterfly Safari. She became co-driver/navigator – showing all the skill of a Greek tanker captain – and manuscript typer, who also learnt the names of several butterflies – Kevin being her favourite.

So, the lover of bucolic pleasures – cricket, Yorkshire pudding and parsnip wine – travelled with the lover of chic-flicks, pasta and alco-pops. The result is one of the funniest books I have read – it is amusing, perceptive and it reflects the way in which down-trodden Page views our wonderful political establishment. Indeed certain incidents experienced during the year-long journey have made him feel even more down-trodden than before. It should have been called *Butterflies, Beauty and the Beast* – but did they succeed in seeing all the British Butterflies on the wing in a single summer during their Great British Butterfly Safari? Read on and find out – it is an arresting tale.

Here's an example from
A Butterfly;
That on a rough, hard rock
Happy can lie;
Friendless and all alone
On this unsweetened stone.

Now let my bed be hard,
No care take I;
I'll make my joy like this
Small Butterfly;
Whose happy heart has power
To make a stone a flower.

W. H. Davies

BUTTERFLY THOUGHTS

IT IS A STRANGE WORLD – a safari for butterflies? I have had many safaris in Africa for non-butterflies. I have seen 'the big five' – lion, leopard, elephant, buffalo and rhinoceros. The camera-clicking of the American tourists at every leopard yawn, and elephant ear-flap, must be almost deafening to a butterfly. I have been charged by lions and elephants and have seen a buffalo stampede; but I have charged at butterflies and seen, not a butterfly stampede – butterflies would find it very hard to stampede, but I have seen many butterflies together – not a stampede, nor a shower, more like a 'flutter' – a 'flutter' of butterflies.

It is peculiar trying to watch butterflies in Africa. Most people go to the Masai Mara or the Zambezi to see 'game'. 'Will we see a kill?' they ask enthusiastically in the Third World; something they would look on with horror in their suburban First World lives. A lion and an antelope on the Dark Continent is considered a holiday highlight, whereas a rustic hunting a rabbit, or a hound chasing a hare represents a return to the dark ages at home. But at home or on holiday, the butterfly is usually overlooked.

On safari I have stopped the vehicle and tumbled from the roof to see a flutter of wings. Butterflies are colour, light and movement. They are fragile and delicate in a hard, hostile world. They are beauty. I have seen them settling on moisture in the sand, on discarded fruit, on scented flowers, on the less welcome deposits in the bush that offer odour not scent; nastiness not nectar, unless you are a butterfly.

At waterholes I have seen silken wings while others have sighed, seeing nothing. As colour has sped across grass and passed without a fear through a tangle of thorns, I have given futile chase. What was it? Did you see it? It was a butterfly. Few people want to see butterflies on safari.

It is the same at home. Butterflies were always there, but I did not see them – really see them. There were bright wings along the hedgerows, on thistles, on dandelions – a flutter in the sun over the bramble blossom.

They were butterflies – but I did not *really* see them.

I saw the *small tortoiseshell* fluttering against the windowpane in a shaft of a warm spring sunlight. 'Hibernation is over,' I was told by my mother. 'Spring is here, help me catch it and let it out.' Soon the rainbow colours would join the violets, primroses, crocuses, daffodils and blossoms of the season. Spring is the season of colour.

All I remember of butterflies is that there were far more of them 'then'. 'Then' was a time of long days, dust, sun, wildflowers along the lanes and lark song in the sky. 'Now' is a time of short days, rush, noise, streetlights, flowerless fields and the relentless march of 'progress'.

It is 'progress' that has been the undoing of the butterfly, and it is 'progress' that has made me want to see butterflies on a safari. I want to see all the British butterflies, in as great a number as possible – and I want to see them all now – in a single year. Fifty-six, fifty-seven, fifty-eight, fifty-nine species of butterfly (who knows how many) even the experts disagree. In woodland, wetland, hay meadow, moorland, mountain, bog, farm, field and forest I want to see butterflies. I want to see each one in a solitary summer, before 'progress' makes the task easier – before poison in the air, land and water removes more beauty from our lives and leaves just thirty species of butterfly. It will be a Great British Safari to see all the butterflies of Britain.

It is fortunate that I do not live in a country called Europe, or a continent called Africa or America. I could not possibly see all the 576 species of European butterfly, the 3,600 of Africa, or the 700 of America in a single year, but I can see all 57 British Butterflies. It will take some luck, much judgement and a lot of help. It is an exciting challenge and I hope I can do it.

It is strange how I now see each butterfly in focus. Not just a series of back-ground wings and colours through the summer. I do still see wings and colours through the summer, but they have become a procession, or pageant of individual species, with each day, week and month from April to September giving a new species – here – there – in Scotland – in Wales – 'Will they be flying?' 'Is it rain-ing?' 'When is it going to stop?' 'The motorway's jammed!' 'How can I get there?'

A butterfly safari in Britain will not be easy, but it is possible. That is the good thing about butterflies – they can be seen everywhere. There are butterflies on the remotest Scottish islands; but there are butterflies to be seen in the innermost of inner cities. I have seen *small tortoiseshells* flying over one of the highest of the Scottish highlands – but I have seen them too in the centres of London, Manchester and Birmingham. It is butterflies that can link the townsman with nature and put him in touch with his country roots. With such a link, the townsman can be drawn closer to the countryman; window-box to rolling acres. Thank you, butterfly, for linking flowers, beauty, wings and people.

Some people treat butterflies as moving flowers. W. H. Davies, the super-tramp-poet, loved butterflies and flowers.

> As butterflies are but winged flowers,
> Half sorry for their change, who fain,
> So still and long they lie on leaves,
> Would be thought flowers again –
>
> E'en so my thoughts, that should expand,
> And grow to higher themes above,
> Return like butterflies to lie
> On the old things I love.

He was a remarkable man – a tramp, a poet and a romantic. As a young man he lost a leg trying to hop on a train, and late in life he lost his heart – he saw beauty in nature, words and love and all three were shown in his poems.

> Now I grow old, and flowers are weeds,
> I think of days when weeds were flowers;
> When Jenny lived across the way,
> And shared with me her childhood hours…

He had a butterfly mind. He came from Newport in Wales. In that drab blot on the Welsh landscape the burghers of urban Wales have erected a statue of their rural poet. It shows a man with a coat over his head. I suppose that someone somewhere laughed all the way to the bank. I am grateful to Newport council for showing the difference between the town mind and the country mind; butterfly thoughts and little thought at all.

It is Gordon Beningfield I blame for my interest in butterflies. He had a butterfly mind too. Because of him – butterflies, colours and background wings have become individual species; with caterpillars, specialist food plants, favoured places, hidden enemies and always in the background 'progress' – a boggy place drained – flowers sprayed – an orchard uprooted – a new town – a planner's dream – a politician's boast – an environmental insult – a butterfly disaster – countryside nightmare.

Butterflies are called by some an 'indicator species'. They indicate the health of the land: when they are present, the land is healthy; when they have vanished – their absence is a warning. Is it poison, pollution, revolution, evolution or is it simply that we no longer care or understand?

I came to understand – standing in a bog. It was April and the sun was out. The cuckoo was calling, the cuckoo flower was flowering. Gordon said, 'There's an orange tip'. From then on, my life changed. 'Look, here,' he said, 'they lay their eggs on cuckoo flowers.'

Within a minute he had found an egg on a cuckoo flower and butterflies became more than wings – they became wings, flowers, plants and seasons. The wings themselves changed too – I did not simply see the odd whites and yellows and peacock eyes. I saw blues and browns, large and small, fast wings, slow wings and wings that opened to absorb the sun. They all linked sun, air, water, flowers and people – yes, indicator species.

Gordon did far more than introduce me to butterflies. He was an artist, a conservationist and a fighter for the country way of life. He turned butterfly illustration into art and countryside art into a crusade.

Although a dyslexic, he became an expert on Thomas Hardy and he introduced me to Dorset and Hardy country. He introduced me as well to Gertrude

Bugler – then an old lady. It was a remarkable feeling, meeting her. It was like meeting history – a figure linking past and present. She had been the beautiful young girl whom Hardy had wanted to play his Tess in the stage version of *Tess of the D'Urbervilles* in London. Mrs Hardy had said that she was not to play Tess – and she did not. But even though well into her eighties it was possible to see what Hardy had seen: her eyes were wonderful – beautiful, full of life, light and laughter.

It is as a thank you that this book and the Great British Butterfly Safari itself are being dedicated to the life, work and memory of Gordon Beningfield.

Part of the proceeds will go the Gordon Beningfield Memorial Appeal towards buying a farm in Dorset; it will be a farm for people, wildlife and agri-'culture'. It will be a farm for butterflies, too.

JANUARY

Monday January 7th

I have seen my first butterfly, but does it count? I found something in my house that I call a 'Hoover'. More accurately it is called a vacuum cleaner. I took it to the spare bedroom and whether it was the noise, a gush of warm air through the opened door or the shock of seeing me doing housework — but a **small tortoiseshell** butterfly began battering itself against the window.

I did not encourage its suicidal behaviour — but took it to the other spare bedroom. There I hoped the lower temperature would help hibernation again. I put the 'Hoover' away quickly after that, on conservation grounds.

I decided that a 'Hoover'-disturbed butterfly cannot be counted as the first species of the Safari, otherwise it would be legitimate simply to turn up at a butterfly centre and tick off the species.

Wednesday January 16th

I wrote to the BBC suggesting that they turn the Great British Butterfly Safari into a television series. It could make an immensely funny and at times intensely frenzied series. That combination could make conservation both entertaining and educational: popular conservation – a green screen with a smile – the BBC will never go for that.

FEBRUARY

THERE WERE SEVERAL warm days in February that felt like the first 'butterfly day'. Daffodils began to flower early, as did the aconites and lesser celandines. Last year I was phoned in February by friends who claimed to have seen **brimstones** and **small tortoiseshells**. However the hedgerows remained deserted.

Wednesday February 13th
It reminded me that I hadn't heard from the BBC. Quite unsurprisingly the BBC had no record of the Great British Butterfly Safari. A girl/lady/woman, whatever is the permissible description in these politically correct times, told me she would phone me later in the day after she had conducted a search.

She did not phone.

Friday February 22nd
Still no telephone call so I wrote to the BBC – enquiring whether the programmes department had been infected with foot and mouth. The BBC does not seem to stand for the British Butterfly Corporation.

MARCH

Friday March 1st

Oh dear. How emotional – a letter from the BBC. The Great British Butterfly Safari has been found – two months later. 'I do appreciate that the diversity of Britain's butterfly population is wonderful … however I am afraid this is not a priority for us on BBC2.' I wonder what is a BBC2 priority? I wonder too how the BBC would dumb–down a butterfly. I suppose with computer graphics the butterflies would be made to speak. 'Oh isn't it wonderful flying along this hedge. Oh no, here comes the wicked farmer and his insecticide spray!' There would of course be no mention of the politics behind the farmer using his insecticide spray.

Tuesday March 12th

A warm day, but still no butterflies; about 300 frogs were working hard at trying to make tadpoles in the pond.

Saturday March 16th

The sun was warm. I could smell spring; there is a smell of grass growing – fused with the scents of yellow flowers – daffodils, narcissus, primroses and forsythia.

I had to go to the bank; an increasingly rare experience for a farmer. Lloyds TSB – they keep going on about improving 'customer service'. 'Improving' seems to mean making customers queue longer – with less staff – meaning larger profits for the bank and more inconvenience for customers.

A quarter of a mile from the bank, reality took over from fantasy. A bright yellow butterfly was flying over bright yellow daffodils: I had spotted a *brimstone* butterfly and the Safari had begun. One down – a mere 56 to go. The *brimstone*, it is said, was the first butterfly to be called 'butterfly' – it was known as the 'butter-coloured fly' – then 'butterfly'.

This safari is not just a matter of ticking off butterflies – like a butterfly twitcher – butterflies are too important for that. Once home – I looked for more. Another male was flying in my garden and another along the road. I felt elated. To make it even better there was a nice fresh otter dropping – 'a spraint' – under the bridge where the brook flows beneath the A603. I was so excited I phoned my friend Sarah in London. At home, it was butterflies and otter droppings – in Hammersmith, she had just had 'lunch' and was playing a card game with the delightful name of 'shithead'. It sounded as if it was an unusually appropriate game for several key members of the BBC.

The excitement didn't stop – a bumble bee flew by late in the day – another first of the spring. Some people say that bumble bees are disappearing, the same as most other things, but we still seem to have reasonably good numbers.

Monday March 18th

It seems that I am becoming a butterfly 'twitcher'. I see wings and I twitch. It is a good thing that butterflies are silent otherwise the twitching would increase by several hundred per cent – sibilating wingbeats the other side of the hedge – or behind you. It would make life very difficult.

There were more wings; another **brimstone** – chased by two house sparrows and then a female chaffinch. It got away easily. I have noticed this chasing before – the early butterflies being chased – presumably as a change from peanuts.

Wednesday March 20th

For some reason I was thinking about hunting – fox hunting – not butterfly hunting – and how if hunting is banned, a whole class of law abiding people will be turned into potential criminals. Then the phone rang – twice. Two neighbouring farms had just been raided by criminals – real criminals – almost certainly by didecoys. Sorry, the name 'didecoy' may be politically incorrect, but that is what we call them in Cambridgeshire. It coincided with the arrival of Sarah to talk about the

summer long Safari and how she could fit it in between chick flicks, pasta parties and alco-pops.

Now we in the country are not against all social change and so I was very happy to let her take me up the pub and buy me lunch. There in the pub car park were more didecoys, selling wine out of the boot of a car at £1 a bottle – they were quite safe, as we have about one police panda car for a hundred villages. Needless to say, the landlord was not amused.

Years ago of course, earlier generations of didecoys were gypsies – living off the land and almost certainly at home in a world of butterflies and flowers. Now they are in a world of transit vans and burglar alarms. But what do you do with a sophisticated young lady from London after you have had a pleasant springtime lunch? (That is another compromise of course. I still call my midday meal 'dinner', except when I am trying to impress.) That's right; I took her to see the frogs and toads copulating in the farm pond; I thought that would be the pinnacle of 'super-cool' behaviour. There too, in the shelter of the hedge, I thought there may be an odd butterfly or two – there were none.

Then it happened again. While we were standing just a hundred yards away from my beloved Daihatsu, watching the underwater behaviour of amorous amphibians, more didecoys with a large screwdriver were trying to make off with my Four Trak. I could not believe it – my faithful motor! The vehicle that was

due to take me to the four corners of Britain, seeing wings and chasing shadows, was in danger of being pinched by hooligans and chased by police cars. I have not moved so fast for years and the didecoys ran off – without the Four Trak. Sarah was not impressed. 'So you think London is bad, do you?' she asked scornfully. 'To me Cambridgeshire seems to be England's crime centre.'

It may be – but at least the Butterfly Buggy had been saved.

Thursday March 21st

The first day of spring – for me it was very memorable. I did not see yellow wings but gold wings – goldfinches, two of them, on my nuts. It is the first time I have ever seen these beautiful little birds swinging on my nuts. I have wondered about ways of luring them in to feed – but now they have found the trick of pecking peanuts. Will they come back and will the message spread?

It was about six years ago that long-tailed tits first came into the garden and swung on my nuts. They started on Gordon Beningfield's in Hertfordshire in the same month. They have been feeding regularly on the nuts ever since and now they have started picking up seeds and breadcrumbs from the ground too.

Strangely, long-tailed tits only started feeding on the nuts of Chris Knights in Norfolk last year. I phoned him about the goldfinches – on this occasion Norfolk was ahead of the game and goldfinches have been dining on peanuts there for sometime.

Saturday March 23rd

False alarm. A *peacock* was seen in the farmhouse garden by Rachael – my sister – I searched but found nothing.

Sunday March 24th

I drove through a dreadful stretch of the old county of Huntingdonshire. It is home for barley barons and boasts the highest percentage of lost hedgerows in the country. Cereals are planted right up to the edges of the fields and most of the hedges that remain are trimmed hard each year. They are low, skin-headed hedges – apologies for the real thing. In the middle of this industrialised 'agro' land I had Sunday lunch with my first cousin once removed and his family.

Duncan is a bald doctor – physician cure yourself! Did he use 'Wash and Go' before it went? In his garden two **small tortoiseshells** flew through in fast circles. So another species seen – what a pity it had to be at Hilton in Huntingdonshire. 'Wildlife? We've got plenty.' That's the usual reaction of the industrial farmer – it's usually untrue. Oh dear – I wish I hadn't seen my first **small tortoiseshells** here.

To make matters worse, I missed an open goal. I know grown men should not kick the footballs of small boys, but I did. It belonged to my little first cousin *twice* removed. But I did and I missed the goal. Balls and butterflies in prairie land – a double whammy.

Monday March 25th

Not butterflies in the sunlight today, but more goldfinches. There, on the peanuts in a farmhouse garden in the Cotswolds were two goldfinches. Their liking for peanuts was described as 'recent'. How does the message travel – and how fast? Do goldfinches have a special song: 'Hey – look out for peanuts'? It is astonishing

– particularly as I hate peanuts. Why do such beautiful birds like such awful nuts? It's not just birds of course; why do apparently normal, well adjusted people like McDonald's burgers; I would rather eat a kitchen roll with salad cream.

Tuesday March 26th

I was almost too amazed to eat my ham for breakfast. More goldfinches on nuts; this time in the middle of Exmoor. So the message has travelled 250 miles. I don't understand it. Over the last four or five years I have sat at the breakfast table of my farming friends Diana and Maurice Scott many times and never seen goldfinches on their nuts before.

Exmoor was looking beautiful – more gold on the high moorland in hot sun – migrating golden plovers in breeding plumage. I suppose they will be moving north over the next few days.

I decided to ride today as an act of support for the ordinary traditional country people of Exmoor. Our lovely Prime Minister, Mr Blair, does not seem to like them. Sarah rode too – at one point appearing to do the breast stroke through a deep, dark bog. To put the matter straight it was the horse doing the

breast stroke with Sarah desperately trying to stay on top. With a delightful covering of black slime, she soon took on the appearance of a rather charming septic tank inspector.

Oh dear; after five hours in the saddle – and three or four trips almost out of the saddle – I could hardly walk. I had not ridden for two years, since researching *The Hunting Gene*.

Wednesday March 27th

Returning from Exmoor, I stopped off at the dairy farm of Tom Morris near Taunton. He is an exceptional man. He wears shorts nearly all the year round and when he talks he becomes emotional about the beauty of the countryside and the way of life he believes is under political attack. He does not hunt and from the way I was walking – pain in every step – I am sure he will not start.

In earlier years, the Countryside Restoration Trust has played cricket on his farm – a wonderful field turned into a superb cricket ground. Sadly, the problems caused by foot and mouth and the need to reduce costs have meant that the cricket ground is now grazing for the cows. What is worse – one of the farm's outbuildings has been taken over by an Australian – making cricket bats!

The sun was hot – it felt like a butterfly day. As we were drinking coffee in the kitchen there were wings outside. Two **peacock** butterflies were flying in the sun. They kept settling on old hawthorn berries on the farm track. They were in good condition with their **peacock** 'eyes' reflecting in the sun. I think I will aim for *fifty-six* species. Three down – fifty-three to go.

Friday March 29th – Good Friday

Oh dear, a telephone call: 'Oh Robin, how is your Butterfly Safari going? I saw a **red admiral** today.' No I haven't seen a **red admiral**; but it was an interesting sighting. It is said that the **red admiral** is a migrant and seldom gets through the winter. If this butterfly was properly identified it must have been a winter survivor.

It is far too warm for the time of year. The Blackthorn is on flower. There is no traditional 'Blackthorn winter' so far – it is as hot as summer.

I walked by the side of the brook at the southern boundary of the farm. The skylarks were singing; a hare seemed to be following a tractor and there were several **small tortoiseshells** and **peacocks** – some flying dizzily – dizzy flight seems to be a feature of those butterflies just out of hibernation. Others were attracted to the clumps of lesser celandine on the banks of the brook. The lesser celandine is a greatly underrated flower. Fortunately, Wordsworth caught its beauty perfectly:

Pansies, lilies, kingcups, daisies,
Let them live upon their praises;
Long as there's a sun that sets,
Primroses will have their glory;
Long as there are violets,
They will have a place in story:
There's a flower that shall be mine,
'Tis the little Celandine …

Ere a leaf is on a bush,
In the time before the thrush
Has a thought about her nest,
Thou wilt come with half a call,
Spreading out thy glossy breast
Like a careless Prodigal;
Telling tales about the sun,
When we've little warmth, or none …

Ill befall
the yellow flowers,
Children of the flaring hours!
Buttercups, that will be seen,
Whether we will see or no;
Others, too, of lofty mien;
They have done as worldlings do,
Taken praise that should be thine,
Little, humble Celandine!

Prophet of delight and mirth,
Ill-requited upon earth;
Herald of a mighty band,
Of a joyous train ensuing,

Serving at my heart's command,
Tasks that are no tasks renewing,
I will sing, as doth behove,
Hymns in praise of what I love!

Saturday March 30th

Oh no, I met a friend outside the village post office. He works for the British Antarctic survey. His interest spreads beyond ice and penguins – yes – to butterflies. He too has seen a **red admiral**, plus a **holly blue** and two **commas**. At home a telephone call advised me that someone else had seen a **speckled wood**.

In the garden all I could see was a honey bee resting on my kitchen wall. I was pleased to see it as they have been hit so badly by the nasty varoa mite – a mite that attacks the larvae of the honey bee.

As I walked *down* the garden path – a butterfly flew *up* the garden path. We avoided a collision – it was a **speckled wood**. Another appeared and they spiralled upwards in a territorial dispute. It is odd how an insect that is always associated

with beauty, fragility and gentleness can actually be aggressive. A *peacock* butterfly flew by, only to be ambushed by one of the *speckled woods*; the *peacock* – the larger butterfly was driven off with little bother.

Four down – fifty-two to go.

Sunday March 31st

In a world full of madness, now comes news of more mass dementia. The Transport Secretary, one Stephen Byers, another north-eastern Blairite, has decided to allow a white horse to be carved into a hillside above Folkestone, close to the entrance of the Channel Tunnel. I suppose it is to give asylum seekers a memorable first glimpse of Britain as they emerge from their container lorries and railway trucks.

The one good thing about Stephen Byers, like most politicians, is that the day after he ceases to be in office his name will be forgotten. In office, he is a disaster and he is known only for his apparent incompetence – rail chaos, misrepresentation and arrogance in such large quantities that it follows him around like a pool of oleaginous slime.

The white horse is an unbelievable act of environmental illiteracy. It is to be hacked into a 300 acre special 'Area of Conservation' famous for its rare chalkland wildlife including the *adonis blue* butterfly and the spider orchid.

To make the situation even stranger the project has been supported by various animal rights 'celebrities' such as Joanna Lumley and the late Spike Milligan, who appear to be affected by the Cuddly Bunny Syndrome. Evidently the *adonis blue* butterfly is not cuddly enough to have 'butterfly rights', and 'animal rights' have very little to do with conservation.

APRIL

Monday April 1st

There was a swallow flitting low among the cows. It is hot enough for summer.

Wednesday April 3rd

It is another wonderful warm day and the may is coming out in April. May blossom should be out in May yet each year now it seems to be earlier. Even so, there are people who claim that global warming is not taking place. Perhaps they should all be issued with dark glasses and a white stick and awarded a PhD in delusion.

At coffee time I was enjoying global warming in the garden. Sarah was here from London, sunning herself, breathing reasonably fresh air and not playing

'shithead'. Suddenly she screamed and rushed from her chair; a **comma** had tried to land on her T-shirt. It is the first time I have ever seen anybody scream and run from a butterfly. I wonder what the butterfly thought. I wonder too if butterflies scream.

This pristine **comma** seemed unaffected by the sudden screech and settled on a bramble leaf absorbing the warmth from the sun. It is another butterfly that lays its eggs on stinging nettles; it also uses hops and willow so it has quite a choice here. The good news is that the **comma** is expanding its range – unlike so many others. It was soon moved on by the aggressive **speckled wood** that suddenly appeared and tried to mug it.

At mid-day a **large white** flopped by – travelling across my garden. There is only wilderness in my garden and so the **cabbage white** was looking for something more ordered, conventional, and edible. The **large white** really does have a floppy flight; I suppose there must be a reason why some butterflies flop rather than fly, but I do not know it. Robert Graves is another who had no idea:

> *Flying Crooked*
> This butterfly, a cabbage-white,
> (His honest idiocy of flight)
> Will never now, it is too late,
> Master the art of flying straight _
> Yet has – who knows so well as I?_
> A just sense of how not to fly:
> He lurches here and here by guess
> And God and hope and hopelessness.
> Even the aerobatic swift
> Has not his flying-crooked gift.

In the afternoon I walked by the brook again on the Countryside Restoration Trust's Westfield Farm. On the overgrown flood plain there was a real flutter of butterflies – **peacocks**, **small tortoiseshells**, **large whites** and **speckled woods** – one swallow doesn't make a summer – do four butterflies make a spring?

Friday April 5th

To Morpeth to speak to members of an endangered species – members of the Morpeth Hunt.

It was an incredible journey north. I left in sunlight with birdsong, butterflies, bursting buds and dripping greens, and drove into winter. By the time I got to Morpeth I had the car heater going; an icy east wind was blowing and the trees were quite leafless. Any self-respecting butterfly would still be locked into hibernation; any not in hibernation would be ex-butterflies – killed by the cold.

They were an interesting bunch of people – angry people. Some had seen all their healthy animals 'contiguously culled' – that means needlessly killed – during foot and mouth. A poet, Catrina Porteus recited her own poem about foot and mouth. I was speaking directly after her and found it so moving that it took me a minute or two to collect my thoughts.

I sat next to a young and beautiful 'painter and decorator'; can I really believe she was a hunting painter and decorator? She smelt of Christian Dior – not paint stripper.

Saturday April 6th

It was colder still in the morning. The cold temperature was matched by the coldness of my thoughts. Just north of Newcastle, an attractive tree-fringed pool gave a winter landscape in the spring. The motorway side gave a bleaker roadscape – in the gutter a dead otter lay in a pool of blood.

Apparently foxes being chased by hounds and horses is a great evil. Wildlife being shredded, minced and maimed on our roads does not require a second thought – all 250 million of them. Some time ago I wrote to John 'Two Jags' Prescott – when his political responsibilities included transport. He is, it seems to me, a second-rate politician whose stomach size matches his ego. I asked him for wildlife speed limits where vulnerable wildlife was threatened by traffic. The exercise was a waste of time, money and ink. I should imagine that he thinks a **comma** and a **large white** are types of car.

The picture of the otter stayed with me all the way home – so did the temperature. It was raw and cold with an east wind that blew through me, rather than round me. The 'Blackthorn winter' had arrived. All butterflies have gone back to sleep.

Sunday April 7th

The first calf has been born during the night – a healthy little bull. Shortly, with the help of a rubber band, it will become a bullock. The mother seemed to object more to the placement of the rubber band than the calf. It simply cuts the blood supply off – turning bull into bullock quite painlessly by removing the bullock's b ... s in two or three weeks. A bullock is a bull without b ... s. Rural vocabulary is so coarse.

The sight of the calf was not painless to Sarah – with the mother nodding her head at close quarters in agitation on one side and the bull, the father nodding his head in excitement on the other, we were caught in a pincer movement. It was almost as dangerous as crossing the road in Hammersmith. I always carry a crook or a stick when the cows are calving; some people may think that this is affectation – it is actually for self-preservation. When the bull started flicking his back legs out skittishly Sarah got so close she almost pushed me towards the angry cow. A whack with the stick brought back normality and security – the whack going to the bull – not Sarah.

The bull is a young bull and the calf is his first. For several minutes he tried to kick it. I had never previously seen such behaviour. I assume as an adult he had never seen a calf before – did he think the small dark animal was a dog? Another whack sent him on his way and no harm was done.

Tuesday April 9th

The sun has come again. The rest of the cows are due to calve in the brook meadows and more swallows have arrived. I spoke to Miriam Rothschild today; at the age of 94 she is a wonderful woman – or is she a lady? She is actually a government-created Dame – so probably I should just say she is a wonderful dame. She was bemoaning the lack of flies. Not many people worry about a lack of flies – but Miriam does. Flies mean food for all sorts of things – including swallows – and she has no swallows either.

In my garden, on a plastic table and chairs at coffee time, I had hundreds of flies sunning themselves. That in itself is odd – what happens when the sun comes out? Sunbathers appear in human form and fly form – the brain size or capacity in both must be about the same.

But then one of the butterflies I had been waiting for suddenly appeared flying fast and high through the buddleia. I shot to my feet – almost spilling my coffee. The little blue butterfly did a circuit of the garden and returned to settle on a bramble leaf. It is a beautiful insect with deep metallic blue wings – as it flew round again the sun kept firing the colour with light. We have so many stunning creatures in poor urban-dominated England, yet their beauty is often overlooked.

Two **speckled woods** were still at the bottom of the garden – flying around one another in ever decreasing circles – I think I would prefer to be a **holly blue**. They have two generations a year – feeding on holly for the first brood and ivy for the second. So why is it not called 'the holly and the ivy blue'? When holly and ivy are in short supply the butterflies also use spindle, dogwood, snowberry, gorse and bramble as the foodplants for their caterpillars.

Wednesday April 17th

Another hot, sunny day, like full summer, not spring. It is the day of the first Countryside Restoration Trust trustees meeting of the year. Jane Wallis came early to look around Lark Rise Farm. She is a founder trustee and has been a major pillar of support and encouragement during the nine years of the CRT's existence. She was once my next-door neighbour. At that time too she was one of Britain's top three-day event riders – winning Burleigh once, coming second once (which was also the European Championship) and riding for Britain. Appearances are deceptive – beneath the girlie smile she must have been tough and brave to be an event rider.

I have two things in common with Jane. We are both worried at the destruction of the countryside by ignorant, urban politicians, and we both hate Tony Blair and his awful wife and we both laugh too much. Sorry – I have three things in common with her. Arithmetic never was my strong point.

The larks were singing and along the boundary hedge between Barton and Grantchester (the home village of the convicted criminal Jeffrey Archer) several **small tortoiseshells**, **peacocks** and **brimstones** were flying. Then came a smallish white butterfly with a flopping flight – the **small white** – lover of cabbages and hated by gardeners.

Eight down, but still no **orange-tip** or **red admiral**.

Friday April 19th

I woke up late. The sun was streaming through my bedroom window, the birds were singing and I felt guilty; I ought to get up. Then I saw butterflies, flying over the lawn; a small yellow one, a white one and another that looked dark chestnut – a **fritillary**? I shot out of bed, only to see a chipmunk and a bluebird. What would come tiptoeing through the grass next; Bambi, or a dew-dappled Paul McCartney? Then I remembered; it was Friday, I was in

America so none of the butterflies would count. The reason why I had still been in bed was because I had just had the equivalent of a 33-hour day. Immediately I had arrived I had been whisked away to supper. I have never eaten in a room full of billionaires and millionaires before. My immediate neighbour was only worth 9 billion – pounds or dollars seems rather irrelevant. They were good company – but how do you explain to such wealth that the CRT could do with a small slice of it?

Spring in Virginia is a very attractive time of the year, almost as pleasant as Cambridgeshire. The trees are full of blossom and there are flowers that look familiar; violets, dandelions, hedge garlic and ground ivy.

But like Cambridgeshire, the Americans are doing their best to ruin it with development gone mad. In Cambridgeshire the madness shows itself in 'new communities' made up almost entirely of assorted little boxes selling at absurdly high prices.

Near one such 'new community', a new McDonald's service area was constructed in old fields, surrounded by high hedges. McDonald's then kindly cut the hedges down so the burger/petrol eyesore could be seen for miles around. Apparently, this form of legalised hooliganism is called 'landscaping'.

The American version is even less subtle. Everything except a few trees are bulldozed for as far as the eye can see. 'What is that going to be,' I asked naively, 'a golf course?' 'No,' came the reply, 'it will soon be part of Washington.'

Being American of course, some of the development involves the direct opposite of the 'little boxes' approach. There were acres of mass-produced mansions, each one with its own manicured acre of lawn. The McMansion has arrived.

My short visit to America was at the invitation of the National Sporting Library in Middleburg. Middleburg is a quiet little country town, the people are polite and friendly and unlike Britain there is hardly any litter. In England Milton Keynes has the distinction of having one of the most unimaginative street names possible with 'Bottledump Roundabout'. Middleburg runs it close with 'Frying Pan Road'.

American car-stickers are distinctly variable ranging from *Brake for Penguins*, to a red, white and blue background bearing the legend *These colours do not run*. Medically this must be diagnosed as 'short-term memory loss'. They have obviously forgotten the Vietnam War already. Some of the American toilets are even more worrying: automatic washbasin taps and automatic toilet flushers — frightening.

The National Sporting Library had invited me to speak, not on butterflies, something far less appealing — that great British fighter for freedom and democracy — Tony Blair.

They were fascinated to hear what he is doing to the British Countryside: destroying farming, driving people from the land, breaking up families and communities, and, of course, attacking rural culture and tradition.

Like me, they were amazed at how he could make grand declarations and assertions in America, following September 11th (2001), while at the same time in Britain his Government is seeking to harass and discriminate against a legitimate minority. They were interested too to hear about the lovely Cherie Blair. I simply told them that she made Hillary Clinton seem 'nice' — they understood totally.

Excitingly, many of those present had seen *One Man and His Dog* on television in America, and they were outraged to hear how it had been dumbed down and I had been sacked for trying to save the programme.

By the time I had finished, they were not surprised to hear that the BBC's Director-General, Greg Dyke, would not see me to discuss the Corporation's attitude towards the countryside, and they all had a much clearer view of life in Britain for country people under the smiling, gleaming, scheming Tony Blair.

Many made promises to come to England to take part in the new Countryside March on September 22nd (2002) — unless it is banned as another

New Labour expression of commitment to the philosophy of 'freedom and democracy'.

Of course, everything in the American countryside is not wonderful. I met a farmer who was no longer able to sell her superb fresh milk for human consumption, because she refused to have it 'ultra-pasteurised, grade A homogenised, with disodium phosphate, sodium citrate and carrageen'. Instead she packages her fresh, pure milk and markets it as 'Kitty Milk'.

Yes, fresh milk for cats, and she is making a small fortune. She must hope and pray that health and safety regulations for felines do not come in.

While in the USA I bought a book for the flight home – the collected stories of *Little Black Sambo* – delightful stories and illustrations that I enjoyed as a small child. They are now considered 'racist' by the politically correct who clearly cannot recognise well-told children's stories when they meet them. It was sold to me in an antiquarian bookshop by a Black American who assured me that she found the stories delightful too. Perhaps if I survive the flight home, I should invite Tony Blair to visit the real countryside – as a sign of forgiveness I'll give him the book to read to dear little Leo.

Monday April 22nd

Homeward bound. If I were a mathematician I would work out the percentage of 'fat' Americans who travel by air. It is hardly surprising the planes have to be 'wide bodied'. I suppose in the States the 'burger belly' is as widespread as the 'beer belly' in Britain. It is fortunate that butterflies don't seem to have the same problem.

The daylight flight over Newfoundland was spectacular – islands, snow fields, sand bars, and yet more islands; it always makes me wonder at the courage of those men in small sailing boats sailing westwards who pioneered the age of exploration. It is politically correct to talk down their achievements – they are now 'wicked colonialists' – they were very brave and often very cold and wet adventurers.

Sitting for hours travelling eastwards over the Atlantic I marvelled at other travellers – ***American monarch*** butterflies. How on earth do they cross the Atlantic on such flimsy wings – with nowhere to rest?

The ***monarch*** is the biggest and arguably the best butterfly to visit Britain – well it would be, wouldn't it, coming from America. Its wingspan is apparently 110 millimetres – which in English is four inches. Even I sound tall in millimetres. It may be the biggest jumbo jet of a butterfly – but I would regard the **white admiral** as Britain's most beautiful – a pleasure that I must not miss in July and August.

The **monarch** is remarkable however – on home territory it travels from Mexico to Canada – breeding as it goes. Then in the autumn it makes an extraordinary migration southwards again of some 2,300 miles – presumably with no time or energy to mate. Once back in Mexico it has huge communal over-wintering sites.

Sadly our transatlantic arrivals usually turn up in September or October in dribs and drabs on favourable winds. With conditions right, they can make the crossing in four days – but why bother? – there is no food plant here and so it is now unlikely that they will ever become 'wicked colonialists', unless they can find an alternative food to 'milkweed', the butterfly burger equivalent for the caterpillars of the **American monarch**.

There are European **monarchs** too, in Spain and the Canary islands, but the experts believe that our incomers are American; I hope some survive the four-day crossing this year.

Tuesday April 23rd

I woke up late. The sun was streaming through my bedroom window, the birds were singing and I felt guilty; I ought to get up. Then I saw butterflies, flying over the lawn; a small white one and a large yellow one. Then there was a knock on the door – it was Eric the postman – it was Tuesday – this must be England.

If this is England, then I have to check to see how many calves have been born in my absence. It's not just a matter of counting them. As our bureaucrats claim to want to cut red tape – they actually manage to produce yards more of it, requiring not one ear tag, but two for every calf; in addition, if it is a male, it needs introducing to the castration ring – a little rubber ring that makes a bullock out of a potential bull. Consequently with three pieces of equipment, a notebook and a pen – the common herdsman needs three pairs of hands simply to deal with each new calf. Then of course there is the stroppy mother; health and safety regulations apparently apply to everybody except farmers having to ear tag their new calves. I have only been tossed once so far and battered several times. It is bad enough when the calves have just been born – but thanks to my American trip there are now new calves several days old. They no longer have wobbly legs – they have frisky legs. Oh dear; there will have to be rugby tackles; clothes covered with cowpats and menacing mothers. The realities of true bumpkinland have little in common with the average townsman's or citywoman's rural dream.

I wonder if butterflies dream? What happens to the butterfly mind between the first autumn frost and the warmth of spring sunshine? Is there butterfly thought; is there feeling; is there memory? What if there are none of these things? Welcome to the world of modern man.

What happens when the warmth of spring turns to 'blackthorn winter' – does the butterfly return to dream or drowse-land and what does it mean to a butterfly to be 'comatose'?

As I climbed the stile thinking of feet to count – warm orange wings floated by. 'Look, a butterfly,' Sarah pointed in the opposite direction as a **large white** waltzed by dreaming of cabbages.

She had missed the first **orange tip** of the spring, but like the lively calves – its wing-beats were not tentative; this was a butterfly several days old, bouncing and buoyant on the warm air.

My interest in counting calves was gone; it was time to count the **orange tips**, and they knew. Fourteen of them appeared in no time – fourteen males – the females have no orange tips to their wings and to the casual observer they get mistaken for **cabbage whites**.

But can a butterfly be casual? Surely there are too many enemies – too many thorns for a casual butterfly. Try chasing a butterfly without a net. Two things will surprise you – their speed, as you stumble through gateways, around bushes and over the ditch – they will be gone – even the *orange tip*, wafting by on the warm wind, they will be gone. And as they go, watch their navigation – how they miss the bramble and the barb on metal wire; how they float over thistle and under thorn, how their fragile wings so rarely tear. It is astonishing; a butterfly at first glance is so uncoordinated and uncontrolled; in reality its changes of direction are nothing short of aerial aerobatics with the *orange tip*, the *comma* and even the floppy *cabbage white* in complete control – precision fluttering.

So if we do not know how butterflies fly; if we do not know how they navigate; if we know nothing of their dreams – do we know whether butterflies fall in love? And if they do, how do they communicate and when? For the *orange tip* butterfly 'lovers lane' must be near the food plant of the caterpillar – cuckoo flower (or milkmaids), and hedge garlic (or Jack-by-the-hedge).

The mating of the *orange tip* butterfly is not a pretty sight. Like all the other butterflies the loving couple make love back-to-back; even the participants can't bear to watch.

I could have watched the *orange tips* all day and there were plenty of their favoured food plants – including a good clump of cuckoo flowers – flowering with no sound of the cuckoo. Instead I had to walk on to count calves, and yes, later in the day I did get covered with cowpats.

Thursday April 25th

Friends and acquaintances still continue to phone – 'Have you seen a *red admiral* yet? I have.' 'How many have you seen so far?' 'Only nine – I've seen eleven.' 'I've seen thirteen.'

'Yes, sorry, only nine.' I am beginning to feel inadequate – should I turn to Valium, soluble aspirin or drink?

Then the telephone rang again and it was Nigel, my right hand-man on the CRT – I shouldn't have answered – here we go again. 'Have you seen a *small copper* yet? I have.' It transpired that Nigel had been to the North Norfolk coast, near to his home, and had seen *small coppers* on the sand dunes at Holkham – oh dear!

'Near the nudist colony?' I asked.

'Right next to it,' he replied. Nigel sometimes wears pink socks – I hope he wasn't wearing them when he saw one of our prettiest butterflies. Sadly the area for naturists at Holkham appears to have been taken over by gay exhibitionists – I suppose in strictly biological terms it does increase the bio-diversity of the North Norfolk coast. Nigel wishes the bio-diversity would decrease, so that he can wear his pink socks without fear.

The **small copper** is an attractive little butterfly with a wingspan of just $1\frac{1}{8}$ inches. Its name does not do it justice – '**small copper**' is just not good enough. It ought to be the 'Duke of Burgundy's polished copper' – because in sunlight it almost shines, or glows – burnished copper. It is also an important little butterfly – it is the skylark of the butterfly world. For years, the skylark was ignored. On a hot summer's day the song of the lark was always there – part of the backdrop of summer. Then gradually the singing drifted into silence – it had almost gone before we had noticed its absence. The occasional lark could still be heard – but its decline crept up on us.

So it is with the **small copper**. Once this little gem of a butterfly was always there – with its three generations in a single summer (four in very hot summers). Its food plants were also common – hence, common sorrel, sheep sorrel and common dock. But gradually, quietly, the old meadows and ditch banks have been tidied up; farm sprays, garden sprays and general pollution have increased. Of course, most people do not regard increases in pollution as their pollution. As the 'two car' family becomes the 'three car', as the lights are left on 'for security', as the garden brochure recommends the use of more slug pellets and moss spray, and of course – 'Don't forget to pull up that dock' – so pollution and the disappearance of the **small copper** 'has nothing to do with us'. The Pontius Pilate syndrome is alive and well and living in suburbia, agribusiness land, the Town Hall and Parliament.

Hearing the **small copper** called the 'skylark of the butterfly world' by Martin Warren of Butterfly Conservation, pulled me up with a jolt. It made me realise that I hadn't seen it for at least two years on our small farm – it had done a 'Skylark'. When we first noticed that the skylark had dwindled, we, and the CRT, did something about it; we now have one of the highest densities of skylarks in East Anglia. But we have rough fields with dock and sorrel; we have a host of flowers and blossom where the butterflies can draw on nectar – so what has happened? Is it drift from farm sprays? They say that the chemicals in 'green' unleaded petrol have turned car exhausts into an 'ungreen' mild insecticide. If you are a **small copper** butterfly, sitting in sunlight, minding your own business, sipping nectar from a bramble flower, with your wings open – how can a do-it-yourself insecticide blown in from the nearby motorway be called 'mild'? When the threat to people is mild (BSE), hysteria breaks out; when the threat to butter-flies is 'mild' silence reigns – apart from 'Unleaded please – fill it up'.

So, pink socks or not – it became a dash to Norfolk, in the hot, unseasonal sun, to see the **small copper**. What a relief – Nigel's butterfly searching socks were not pink – but yellow, to match the sand. They matched the **brimstones** in his garden as well. There were **holly blues** too – dancing in and out of light and shade.

We travelled in convoy; 'Oh,' Sarah exclaimed, as something splattered on the windscreen of the butterfly buggy. 'It was a butterfly. That's one way of seeing them at close quarters.'

Holkham is wonderful. In winter it is wild – a place of wind, surf, deserted sand and geese – thousands of them. Today it was so warm – the air was redolent with the scents of spring – fresh growth, new leaves, the bursting blooms of gorse and pine – all stirred – not shaken – in a warm breeze.

The pines and dunes of Holkham differ from Hammersmith – the lack of conveniences can be very inconvenient – consequently Sarah had to go into the undergrowth for a lesson in bush ducking – exposing cheeks of white flesh to the ravages of early midges and mosquitoes. Conservationists might one day con-serve midges and mosquitoes – they too have to live. We walked on; voices approached; Sarah's duck, we assumed, became a panic stricken low squat, as two giggling young men minced by – we were approaching the dunes.

Almost immediately we were in the dunes. Nigel shouted – 'Here's one'. Thank goodness he was referring to butterflies. His wife Barbara shouted 'Here's another'. The **small coppers** were obviously doing well in the valleys of sheltered sand away from ploughs, cars and slug pellets. Then came another shout 'What are these?' On the stems of marram grass were more butterflies, pristine and newly emerged – **common blues** – two species for the price of one – the Safari has leapt forward to a total of eleven.

Again the name is rather unfair – the **common blue** certainly does not look 'common'; it is a deep sky blue. If seen in another part of the world it would be regarded as exotic – but here, it is seen as 'common' or not seen at all.

From the top of the dunes under a cloudless sky it was a fine sight: acres of almost deserted sand and then the blue sea fusing with the blue sky – oh dear, and then a sign. 'You are advised that the beach beyond this point may be in use by naturists.'

There was no 'may be' about it – it was in use by naturists! What was going on under one large umbrella is anybody's guess; count the feet and divide by two. An almost naked man in a seafaring hat kept watch from a sandy hillock – 'Hallo Sailor'. Shielding his eyes from the sun he kept looking into the horizon – was he saying 'I see no ships', or more likely: 'I am only scouting for boys'?

For couples with young children – or even people with no children, the walk past Holkham's naturists has become an unpleasant experience. It is almost like running a gay gauntlet.

Inevitably the politically correct say that this is society moving forwards. In reality it is striding backwards into history 3,000 years – Sodom, for Gommorrah we die.

It is quite interesting – fish in the North Sea are changing sex; male polar bears are losing their potency – not through the cold – and even some male seagulls in the Pacific are favouring other male seagulls. The reason given is that pollution – heavy metals, etc. – is causing a disturbing change and the change worries both scientists, and, superficially at least, politicians. Could that same pollution be affecting the Holkham frolickers? Sadly we will never know; those who rule our minds would never allow research that showed 'social change' to be caused by pollution rather than 'liberal enlightenment'.

At least some of the **small coppers** in the dunes appeared to be unaffected by pollution or social change – as a consequence there will be more generations of this attractive butterfly later on in the summer.

Sunday April 28th

Sarah was supposed to be returning from London today. The telephone rang and it was Sarah on a mobile in a state of panic: 'Robin – Where am I?'

How should I know from my living room where she was? Apparently she was travelling on the M25 but did not know where she was or which direction she was going in. Thank goodness she came after Christopher Columbus and Captain Scott. She would not make a very good migrating butterfly either. Butterflies do not have map-books, sign posts, or mobile phones – but they still manage to find their way from North Africa and Southern Europe; Sarah cannot find her way from London to Cambridge.

I suppose some butterflies get blown here from America. But a butterfly can surely be excused for being picked up and floated eastwards in a gale. Can Sarah be excused for driving anti-clockwise instead of clockwise around the dreaded M25? Her rust bucket of a Ford would never be lifted by the wind – dustcart yes – but never by the wind, nor even by a gale – so how can she get lost?

Most butterflies seem to know North, South, East and West – but some women seem unsure about which is left and which is right. Right and wrong, yes – right and left – no. I advised Sarah to pull off the motorway and look at the sun – or a map. She chose the map and arrived two hours late for Sunday 'lunch' – dinner.

MAY

Thursday May 2nd

Somewhere different – somewhere new – the Badminton Horse Trials. The reason is simple – a different place – a different time – I might just see some fresh butterflies in Gloucestershire rather than Cambridgeshire. It would be good to get as many under my belt as early as possible just in case the weather changes for the worse and the butterflies disappear. The **green veined white** is supposed to have been flying since mid–April but I have not seen a hide nor hair of it, yet alone a scent or sound. Do butterflies have hide or hair? The answer is yes – they certainly have body hair, both male and female, and (I will try and remain tasteful) they also have hair on the lower abdomen – to retain heat – which butterflies get from the sun. They don't have hide – but an exo-skeleton – a hard case on the outside of their bodies, with the muscles and organs on the inside – if only I had an exo-skeleton I would always look thin.

And what about scent or sound? I have certainly never heard butterflies talking or even whispering – so how do they communicate? How does a butterfly say: 'Hello I'm here!'? How does a butterfly say: 'HELLOOO – OVER HERE'? If rare butterflies cannot communicate – they will become even rarer butterflies. They certainly cannot gossip or even talk as they don't have jaws – what a peaceful life male butterflies lead with nobody to say: 'now listen!' Instead of jaws they have a proboscis – a long tube-like structure for taking nectar from flowers. The butterfly can have a surprisingly varied diet – a sort of honey and fruit salad – nectar, sap from wounded trees, honeydew from aphids and the juices of fruit – fresh and rotten – hence they suck but they cannot chew; a chewing butterfly would definitely lower the tone.

But that is not all – scent and sound? Butterflies have a wonderful sense of smell – so rare butterflies can after all find other rare butterflies, and hungry butterflies can find food. With their bobbled antennae, not only can they smell but they can also feel vibrations – hear? That is the big difference between moths and butterflies – moths have no bobble on the end of the antennae.

But these remarkable creatures are even more remarkable – as they can also taste and smell through their feet and through the *palpi* – I hope I'm not being too academic – *palpi* are organs at the base of their antennae.

I was at Badminton without antennae or *palpi*, selling my books on the stand of the Countryside Alliance and between sales I was thinking of butterflies, mapping out the year long Safari in the gap between my ears.

As I planned I was approached by a most attractive human butterfly – Tracey – not a very good name for a butterfly. But what's in a name? In every other way she is like a butterfly with a definite butterfly mind – skipping, fluttering, settling – travelling from one subject to the next. 'Come to supper!', she said – that sounded like a good idea – I hope we have serviettes – multi-functional knives and forks can be so much more difficult to eat with than a single proboscis.

Another attractive female butterfly stood at the back of the stand looking bored. I phoned her on her mobile, 'Richard Burge here (the C.A.'s Chief Executive). Where's my car – how will I get from the station to Badminton?' She went white and stood to attention – why stand to attention – it was not a visual phone? In butterfly terms he was clearly the **red admiral** while she was the lowly **cabbage white**. Oh dear – at this rate she would soon need Valium – so I walked up to her – still on my phone. I didn't realise until then that **cabbage white** butterflies could become violent.

Sarah couldn't make Badminton and so Nigel was butterfly adjudicator and also distributor of CRT literature – we stayed with the Farquhars – one of the most famous hunting families in the country – with one of the most difficult names – for me at any rate – to pronounce. The two words I have problems with in life are 'Farquhar' and 'entrepreneur'. Does everybody have this problem? A friend cannot say 'binoculars': he can only say 'binnocunocunoculars'. Every other word in his vocabulary he can say perfectly but not binnocunocunoculars. And I can only say – if pressed – Farahaquarquaquaqua – so I call him Ian. He is very good company and joint Master and Huntsman of the Duke of Beaufort's hunt – a living hunting legend.

I saw no real butterflies – but enjoyed Tracey's company at supper – and that of her husband, Bunter. Why are nicknames so hurtful – the fictional Billy Bunter was a glutton. The real Bunter seemed of normal body mass to me and he ate as daintily and tidily as if he had a proboscis. Why are some people so tall – even sitting down? Bunter was almost taller sitting than I was standing – is it genes? Or was I deprived of orange juice as a child?

We wined and dined well and put the world to rights. On this occasion, the conservationists and butterfly-lovers won – Tracey had given us a good evening. I wonder if there is another Marchioness in the world – not just Britain – called Tracey, Marchioness of Worcester.

We drove back in convoy to the Captain's house. I couldn't believe it; the bad man and his lovely wife Pammy-Jane had forgotten we were there and locked us out – locked out by a living legend.

Friday May 3rd

It's my birthday. I woke up at 4 o'clock with a cock crowing near my car. I was not just cold, I was freezing – I wonder if Nigel's pink socks in his car are warmer than my grey socks in mine. Ian Farquarquarquar opened the door at 8 o'clock and looked startled – he let us in to warm up in time to leave at 8.15 for another day of selling books.

The day was spent thawing and dozing – if a **green-veined white** and a **red admiral** had settled on each cheek I would not have noticed.

Wednesday May 8th

'To Wayills Boyo.' If things ever get desperate for Sarah I don't think she will get a job as an impersonator. Her 'Wayills Boyo' accent sounds exactly like her Pakistani, Irish, Italian and cockney accents.

Going to Wales to see butterflies? Wales is the last place I would expect to look for butterflies – unless Welsh butterflies wear snorkels and carry umbrellas. The main butterfly on this sortie is the **pearl-bordered fritillary** – all the **fritillaries** only fly in the sun and so is it wise to drive west – to Wayills Boyo? I must have more faith – Simon Spencer lives in Wales; Simon Spencer loves butterflies; Simon Spencer wears a beard and sandals – he must know what he is talking about.

I drove along the A14 – two lanes each way east to west – designed to frighten. Sarah listened to 'Vibe FM', electronic Beethoven for the tone deaf, while 'doing' her nails. A slogan sprayed on a bridge read: 'Kick them out – time for a change'; it has been there for years – but yesterday – today – and tomorrow it is most appropriate.

At least some people are lucky to have a bridge on this death-trap of a road – every so often there are signs pointing across the middle of the carriageway saying 'Bridlepath' and 'Footpath' and a gap in the crash barrier shows where the foolhardy, or the demented, are supposed to cross one of the busiest trunk roads in rural Britain. In urban Britain the inhabitants next to dangerous roads get bridges, in much of rural Britain they get precisely nothing.

'Vibe FM' throbbed on – Sarah moved on from nails to eyelashes, turning black to a spectacular vivid blue. It was very difficult to keep my eyes on the road: I felt like Charles Darwin trying to study the behaviour of a completely new species, *Girlie urbanimus*. Sarah was having exactly the same problem, but she was studying *Rusticus geriatricus bumpkindulae*.

By the end of the M50, on the border of Wales, we switched seats. We were going to Welsh butterfly land via the Chepstow Countryside Race Day, where I had to say a few words of encouragement to beleaguered Welsh farmers, hunters and country people. A snooze before arrival would set me up for lunch – so Sarah could drive the Butterfly Buggy through the valleys to Chepstow Race Course, boyo.

Snooze, turned to nightmare – to white-knuckle ride. We were late and suddenly Sarah was transformed from gentle butterfly safariist to manic girl-racer. Two minutes after beginning to snooze we seemed to swerve left – my eyes opened to see a telegraph pole rush past – six inches from my nose. 'What's up?' she asked, 'Everything's alright – go back to sleep.'

I arrived at the Racecourse exhausted – drained. I had been very brave – I hadn't screamed. We were put on a table which included David Broome – the old showjumper, with gold medals for just about everything. 'That's David Broome,' I whispered. 'Who?' Sarah whispered back. 'He's famous.' 'Is he?' I felt like a history teacher.

Suddenly the woman on my left stopped talking – and eating. She went white and begun to tremble. Oh no, what had I done – or said? Why don't I just shut up and sit quietly. What had I said? Oh yes, old jokes about Sarah's driving: 'she knows the difference between right and wrong, but not left and right'. No, it couldn't be that surely? 'She drove worse than a one-legged lesbian' – no it couldn't be that either, my neighbour had two legs.

I plucked up courage and grovelled, 'I'm sorry – have I offended you?' 'No, no it's not you', she whispered, 'it's that!' She pointed to her plate – and there, relaxing in her broccoli, was one of the biggest caterpillars I have ever seen – dead or alive. I thought the broccoli had been slightly underdone – the caterpillar looked rather over-done. If only I knew what species – could I count a pre-butterfly? It was so big that I do not think it was British. Perhaps it was an asylum-seeking caterpillar. Richard Burge spoke first. 'It's really good being here at Cheltenham,' he said; have another drink Richard. I thought I had better support all those with short-term memory loss so I started, 'It's really good being here at Great Yarmouth'.

I like the rural Welsh. They enjoyed their afternoon – but just in case there were still one or two wild Welshmen in the border country, we retreated to Usk – to Usk Castle – a castle that still has battlements – although some of them have fallen to the ground.

Rosie and Henry Humphreys live in Usk Castle – the falling down part dates back to 1100 and the Normans – the new – where Rosie and Henry live – dates back to 1400. Henry has repaired some of the battlements so he can sit high up above Usk to watch the sun sink down, as the gin trickles down. He has also done up a room in one of the towers where he has installed a water bed – very Norman. The water bed had roughly the same movement as Sarah's driving – a night on that and I would have been sea-sick.

Supper – was really very Norman – wine, laughter and wild boar – the only thing missing was song. Later in the year Henry intends to have a Revolting Peasants' Party where the singing will be done by the 'Wurzels' – far too good for 'Vibe FM'. Their song *I've got a Brand New Combine Harvester* has almost become the anthem for rural Britain. They will be joined by Granny Smith – not a wise old rustic woman, or even a singing apple – but another group whose notes reach the parts that 'Vibe FM's' semi-quavers never reach.

The sun went down in the west sinking into a bank of cloud coming in from the west – oh no.

Thursday May 9th

The sun came up in the east – but I could not see it. It was light fog or thick mist – our first, serious, butterfly day was not looking too promising.

Sarah was dressed up for butterflies – with her butterfly eyelashes and brown knee-length boots with their two-inch heels: 'Shut up', she said, 'they are not shag-me boots – they are ordinary boots, just right for the countryside.' What? Shag-me boots? I can feel a new book coming on – I think I will call it *The Origin of Species*.

Shag-me boots are apparently knee-length boots with thin high heels – worn by slappers – so there I have it – education is a wonderful thing.

As the morning moved on, the mist thinned and lifted higher and higher –

'is that a shaft of sunlight?' Rural Wales is a beautiful place with the border country being more gentle than the north – and the more urban south – there are valleys with oak woods and streams with rocky beds – there are meadows – stone walls – farms – and then there is Welshpool.

Welshpool was once an attractive market town – until the planners found it and planned its heart away. Who trains planners? From the end product the word has to be *train*, rather than *educate*. Now the dominant feature of most British towns is not the church or market place, it is the supermarket and car park and nearly all the supermarkets look the same. Nearly all the town centres in Britain look the same – planned the same – sound the same – smell the same – grid-locked the same. Hit the one-way system – twice round the bunker of the municipal buildings – weave in and out of the rival supermarkets – to the multi-storey car park – and that is town-centre Britain – homogenised – traumatised – vandalised and twinned with Aix-les-Bains.

We left the Butterfly Buggy in the supermarket car park while we sat in the bar of the Royal Oak, waiting for the sun to come. 'They said it would come,' Simon assured us looking at Sarah's non-shag-me boots. We ate sandwiches slowly and sipped our drinks waiting for the light – butterfly light – 'They are flying – I saw it two days ago – but we need the sun.' It suddenly grew lighter and brighter. Sips turned to gulps and we followed Simon's rust bucket out of the town at a vigorous rattle.

We stopped in a wide, low valley – full of greens – light, dark and medium. 'Are you changing your boots?' Simon asked as Sarah clattered and staggered across the road. She didn't change her boots.

We were walking across the field and climbing up the valley side – through lush grass towards a fence and hedge of thorn and nut – hawthorn and hazel – dividing field from moor – grass from bracken. A white butterfly flew along the hedge – through the hedge and into the field. Henry Ford claimed one shade of black; butterflies claim several shades and styles of white – producing **large white**, **small white**, **green-veined white**, **wood white** and **marbled white**.

'**Green-veined white**' Simon identified without even unfurling his net. Yes, it was a **green-veined white** – *number twelve*. As its name suggests, the **green-veined white** has a network of what appears to be olive green veins – another green – on its wings. The **green-veined white** must not be called a **cabbage white** – as the caterpillar never eats garden cabbages – only members of the wild cabbage family such as charlock and garlic mustard.

We squeezed through the fence and hedge – Sarah's heels catching twigs and wire – if she had been a horse it would have been four faults – but at least there were no signs of a refusal.

Immediately flying across dead and winter-bent bracken I saw small wings – beautiful wings – green wings – another green – metallic green – wings I had never seen before. They landed wings-together; what a stunning, perfect little butterfly with a wingspan of just $1\frac{1}{8}$ inches – a **green hairstreak**. Apparently it is widespread in much of Britain – so why hadn't I ever seen this glowing, green beauty before? It is widespread, so it is said, because unlike so many butterflies its caterpillars are easily pleased – they are not limited to just one food plant but will dine out on no fewer than ten – including gorse, broom and rock rose on the moor, and the dogwood and bramble next to the moor. Dogwood, bramble and buckthorn? Cambridgeshire should be full of this remarkable little butterfly.

'Here we are,' shouted Simon as he ran through the bracken, swirling and sweeping his net – with beard, glasses and flailing arms he looked like a manic, mad, Muslim cleric loose on the hills, 'Wild Butterfly Bin Laden', bent on mass butterfly-destruction. 'Got one.' There it was – a **pearl-bordered fritillary** – a rich, russet brown with black patches and blotches – of the eight true British **fritillaries** (excluding the **Duke of Burgundy fritillary** which isn't a **fritillary**) five of the caterpillars eat the leaves of dog violet as their main food plant. Consequently a decline in the number of violets has led to a decline in the number of **fritillaries**. Simon flicked his net and the butterfly was free and unharmed. From the path we could see more – fast flying and almost glowing in the sun. Occasionally one would pause to take in sunlight through open wings – or feed from the flowers of bugle and bluebell. Two decided to mate, and back to back they loved each other, with butterfly passion.

Sunlight – and three Welsh butterflies, new butterflies, had been seen in no time at all: 'Don't say where we are,' Simon pleaded. 'This is such a special place in Wales, we don't want to take any risks.' That was quite safe, Sarah had no idea where she was, neither had I.

The pure sunlight was turning to haze in the unexpected heat: 'Come on let's see some more.' The rust-bucket rattled off towards England – and we followed. Sarah's lucky eyelashes had certainly worked – we wound our way out of Wales and into Shropshire.

We stopped at the overgrown entrance of a small disused quarry – Llanymynech Quarry. 'I thought you said we were in Shropshire?' I queried. 'Only the Welsh could have a name like that.' 'We are definitely in England,' Simon assured us, 'Shropshire — the Welsh exported a lot of I's to Shropshire'. 'And y's Boyo,' added Sarah as she tripped over a stone.

On a heap of shattered limestone, the spoil from earlier quarrying, there were quick — almost moth-like wings — small wings. The butterfly-moth landed — wings open, taking in warmth from above, from the sun, and warmth from below from the heated rock. 'There you are,' Simon enthused, 'a *grizzled skipper*.' What a pretty little butterfly to have such an ugly name. 'Oh it's sweet' — Sarah was in danger of becoming as enthusiastic as Simon.

The chocolate-brown butterfly had a delicate fringe of wing dots of pristine white — with a secondary fringe of grey 'grizzled' hairs. The caterpillars eat the leaves of wild strawberry, cinquefoil and silverweed — while the butterflies suck and sip nectar from the lovely lesser celandine.

Other butterflies flew, flopped and flitted — a *small tortoiseshell*, several *large whites*, a *brimstone* and several more dizzily flying *grizzled skippers*. And what's that? Another butterfly — a larger butterfly — settled with wings open on the warm rocks. *The wall* loves resting on warm, south-facing rock, bricks and stones on a sunny day — hence its name — *the wall*.

'It's early yet — but on a warm day — after a warm spring we might even see another,' Simon said in anticipation. He made off over shattered limestone that moved underfoot; it was made even more lethal by long, trailing tangles of bramble. Sarah followed, with all the elegance of a tight-rope walker about to fall off the rope. 'There it is,' Simon shouted, and pointed in triumph — verging on hysteria, 'the *dingy skipper*.' What an unfair name — dingy, no — attractive, yes — the sixth new species of the day. I thought it was exceptionally beautiful — mottled browns with a fringe of grey hair around the hind wings — *dingy skipper* — certainly not.

Butterflies at first glance have two wings. But on second glance have fore wings and hind wings that overlap, making four wings. They fly with the aid of a number of flat scales or plates — modified hairs — that slot in place and overlap — rather like slates on a roof — but not so heavy — and much quieter.

Oh dear — the males of several species have a number of scent scales on the wing — and so when they flap, they wing-waft their body odour, hoping to attract a mate — 'Smell me; I'm rare; I'm over here; help me be a happy *dingy skipper*.'

It was quite a steep climb to the top of the quarry — over short grass with Sarah's non-shag-me boots threatening to become her slide-me or break-my-ankle boots at every step and stumble.

From the top, Shropshire appeared in a sun-glowing haze, features half hidden and out of focus – a warm landscape trying to hide. We had been so lucky, six butterflies; and one – the **dingy skipper** – not supposed to be on the wing until the fourth week of May at Llanymynech, boyo.

'What's that?' Simon rolled over pointing to another butterfly – a large, dark butterfly, flying low and fast away from us – before returning and flying in a long, low circle right over us. 'It's a **red admiral** – hill topping – displaying and guarding its territory.'

A migrant from Southern Europe? If it really was a migrant it had flown a long way by the ninth of May. As the **red admiral** hill-topped, Sarah hill-bottomed down the steepest slope to prevent instant death. Later in the year she is going to Kilimanjaro – if she hill-bottoms on her posterior down that, for 19,342 feet, how long will her descent take? I hope her non-shag-me boots will be in the dustbin by then.

Before the long haul back to Cambridgeshire we found a little post office-cum-tea room. Tea and biscuits for three while odd customers came in for stamps. What an excellent hazy day of seven butterflies – if we keep it up the Great British Butterfly Safari will take no time at all.

We said goodbye to Simon – what a good, nice man – a man devoted to butterflies; 'See you in July – you must come again to see the **high brown fritillary** – Sarah – get some decent boots.'

It had been a long, hard day – Sarah took her boots off – I opened a window: the Butterfly Buggy, a *Dai*hatsu – could almost be a Welsh car.

Sarah started to snooze: 'I enjoyed today Robin, but I think I wore the wrong kind of boots.'

I kept awake by listening to 'Vibe FM'.

Sunday May 12th

Up early today to get to Dorset to speak at a 'Jubilee May Fair' held by the Campaign for the Protection of Rural England, before going on to the Isles of Scilly. However, to start with I had to deliver Sarah to Cambridge station. She is suffering from 'big city withdrawal symptoms' and needs topping up with the smell of pavements, petrol fumes and alco-pops. She also needs to go to the hairdressers. Butterfly hunting can cause havoc with your split ends.

She has also learnt that if you wear good, clean clothes as you clamber through fences and over old quarries trying to see **pearl-bordered fritillaries** and

dingy skippers, everything becomes dingy, even dirty. The secret of successful, sartorial country living is to wear dirty old clothes from the outset, then there is no need to consider fashion or the advantages of a medium hot wash.

It was a pity that she went, as it was a long day doing all the driving, and speaking, to Dorset and beyond; but a woman's got to do what a woman's got to do. At least it meant that I didn't have to listen to junk pop music as I drove – I could listen to junk cassettes instead. The first was by Jethro Tull – not the great agricultural reformer of the 17th Century, but a bald second division 'sixties pop singer. I had the privilege of hearing him live two years ago. He retains his pop image by drawing his few remaining hairs together in a ponytail. There but for the grace of Vosene go I.

I must be in need of some sort of psychiatric help, as the other cassette was also by Jethro – Jethro the Cornish comedian, whose characters come from St Just. Oh dear – what has become of me on long journeys? My poor old mother must be turning in her grave. I suppose the reason for listening to the two Jethro's is that I find them less offensive than listening to the News and hearing the pronouncements of our great politicians.

I usually accept few speaking invitations during the summer – an English summer is too beautiful, fragile and fleeting to be spent in village halls, conference centres and dining rooms, shouting the odds. I accepted on this occasion because it was Dorset, it was a worthwhile organisation and I do want the Countryside Restoration Trust to get a farm in Dorset as a living memorial to Gordon Beningfield. At the May Fair there were several officials of the Thomas Hardy Society, mixing happily with the madding crowd. They sang Gordon's praises long and loud and they were happy to say that Gertrude Bugler's sister was still alive and well and living in the next valley – an astonishing living, literary link.

The fair was at the village of Warmwell, close to Dorchester; at events like this I like to spread the message of the CRT, sell books, and, this year, see butterflies. It was held on the lawn of a mini-country house, in a winding, low, lush valley of many greens.

Almost immediately I set my books out on a table, a middle-aged man came up to me. 'Oh dear, I wanted a copy of your book *The Hunting Gene*.' I had not omitted the tome for reasons of political or conservational correctness; I had simply forgotten to get it out of the car. As I returned from the car park with a bundle of the forgotten books, an ear-ringed man with shaven head, long shorts, a short wife and a ring through his eyebrow was leaving. 'Are you coming back?'

the gatekeeper (man not butterfly) asked. 'Certainly not!' he replied, 'not while you've got pro-hunting scum like him here.' He pointed at me.

So having travelled nearly 200 miles, simply to say a few words defending the countryside and to promote the Memorial Appeal of my long lamented friend, I was called 'scum'. What a strangely intolerant country Britain is becoming. If you are gay, Muslim, or disabled you are welcomed into multicultural, caring Britain. If you are a traditional countryman you are reviled, discriminated against and in this case, insulted. If only I was a sex change, lesbian lorry driver then the politicians and the broadcasting media would love me – but then I'm not, and they don't. Sadly Mr Scum failed to realise that some butterflies love scum; the mixture of liquid and odour can become irresistible. I hope the *purple emperor* butterfly regards me as scum in July, then it will be much easier to see.

By the time I went into the marquee to do my stuff it was hot. I told them many things about the demise of farming and the politics involved in killing off the countryside, and they seemed to appreciate it. My ten minutes included two stories – one true and one false – which is which?

When Nick Brown MP was Secretary of State for Agriculture we lost over 50,000 farmers and workers in two years. The lovely Mr Blair then, using his well-known sense of humour, moved him from farming and made him 'Minister for Work' – true or false?

Then, to identify with the farmers under her, the new Secretary of State, Mrs Beckett bought 50 laying hens to look after. Within a week they were all dead – she had planted them too deep. Fortunately the people of Dorset seemed to regard politicians in exactly the same way as I do and laughed at both brief stories. So although the Dorset people, except one – were happy – I only saw one butterfly – a male *orange tip* – I must hope for better things to come.

From Dorset the sun slowly faded, heat – to haze – to watery sun with the promise of rain. I didn't want it to rain. I wanted to see the Isles of Scilly in sun. The point of the journey was simple. The Isles of Scilly have become the Mecca in Britain for 'twitchers'. A 'twitcher' is simply a person who twitches when he or she sees or hears wings – birds' wings. Once the owner of the wings is identified, a tick is put by the species name and the search for the next bird begins. Well, it is already clear that I have become a butterfly 'twitcher' and so it seemed right to go to the home of twitching.

As I travelled through Dorset and Devon and on into Cornwall, the promise of rain turned into wet reality. Banks of heavy menacing cloud rolled in from the sea – the wind increased from gentle summer breeze to wild Atlantic gale and unless the weather improved, it looked as though I would stand more chance seeing the Archbishop of Canterbury in Mecca than I would a butterfly on the Isles of Scilly.

Confirmation of just how deep into Cornwall I had travelled came with a sign to St Just. If this is Jethro country there is nothing to laugh about.

At Penzance, huge waves were thundering onto the beach and great columns of spray were rising where the harbour wall was being pounded by the sea. At one time one of the best fishing fleets in the world sheltered behind the Penzance Harbour wall – then our fishing rights were given away to Europe – mostly to Spain – by arrogant politicians more interested in their own short-term egos than the long-term wellbeing of the fishing communities they were destroying. As a consequence, most of the boats currently in the Penzance harbour are lifestyle pleasure yachts.

Now the same arrogant politicians want to give Gibraltar to the Spaniards as well. Self-determination is for the Third World – like the lovely democratic President Mugabe of Zimbabwe – not for British people or people bound to Britain through both history and treaties.

Even the hotel on the seafront was being battered by its own palm trees. This journey could be a butterfly twitch too far.

Monday May 13th

Prospects from the dining room looked bleak. Huge waves topped with white crashed in from a turbulent sea. Rain battered the window – the wind battered the palm trees, and the thick banks of cloud showed more shades of black and grey than I could have imagined. Henry Ford claimed there was only one shade of black – how do Americans get it wrong so often?

Prospects from inside the dining room were even bleaker. I swear the scram-bled egg had been made in a cement mixer. How come that my old departed mother, who only had cookery lessons from her mother, could make scrambled egg that melted in your mouth; yet trained chefs can only make scrambled eggs to lay bricks with. There also seems to be a strict rule in British hotels: 'You must eat rubbery toast with the crusts cut off every single morning'. I asked for two rounds of brown bread. I received two rounds of rubbery white toast with the crusts cut off.

I did not think the helicopters would fly or could fly. How could a machine that I could not even spell, with 20,000 moving parts fly in a storm? Certainly butterflies with about ten moving parts would not be flying. But how many moving parts does a butterfly have when flying, and are the legs counted as moving parts – some butterflies have six walking legs. Others have only four walking – with two becoming redundant, merely ornaments, rather like many city dwellers whose shoulders and biceps appear to have become redundant due to lack of physical work or activity. I wonder if that is the reason for the delightful Mrs Beckham's shoulders and arms – or lack of them – or is it genetic?

Once in the helicopter my survival strategy took over – women and children to the rear and I got a single seat next to an emergency door. In reality of course that probably means that in the event of an emergency I would be hit by one of the rotor blades first. With increasing noise and vibration, the beast took off. I am always amazed how these large helicopters take off anyway – but in a storm? My tiny mind cannot comprehend. I could easily get like the Arsenal footballer Dennis Bergkamp, who refuses to fly. So if ever Arsenal want me to play for them I hope they bear that in mind.

We were soon being buffeted in a world of grey. In the Cairngorms one year I found myself in a 'white out', which focused the mind. This was a 'grey out' in which I was totally unfocused – I could do nothing – my fate was entirely in the hands of another.

How do butterflies manage in conditions like this, to become migrants? As migrant butterflies do reach the Scillies I hoped the **painted lady** had arrived ahead of the storm. But in any case, in storms like this how do small, fragile butterflies breathe and navigate? Breathing is easier for them: gales and high winds affect my asthma – luckily for butterflies they don't have lungs – which also means of course that butterflies can't smoke – even if they wanted to. So instead of 'breathing', 'respiration' takes place through a branching system of air tubes

called trachea. They are open to the air at pores in all sections of the body and once inside they divide repeatedly until oxygen is taken to all parts and organs of the body.

I think that I would find such a system far more convenient – doing away with asthma, bronchitis, breathlessness and most importantly, snoring. That is why I have never found a butterfly at night – they do not snore – they cannot snore. For *Homo sapiens* as a species, and the British branch in particular, such a system of respiration would have one other great advantage – it would at last get oxygen to the brains of politicians.

So that is how butterflies breathe – but how do butterflies navigate? The answer is simple; nobody seems to know, except the butterflies themselves. I will have to ask the great Miriam Rothschild as she knows as much as anybody.

When they decide to cross a sea, is their great journey instinctive or do they plot a course? And how does the **painted lady** fly to Britain from the Atlas Mountains in North Africa and the **red admiral** fly from the Mediterranean? Their journeys must be made in daylight, as butterflies are stimulated by the warmth of sunlight – that rules out navigation by the stars – a gift rightly or wrongly attributed to birds. But why do they want to migrate anyway?

Continental *large* and *small whites* – *cabbage whites*, top up our resident populations – presumably because our cabbages are so much tastier than those from France – but the *painted lady*, *clouded yellow*, the *monarch* and the *Camberwell beauty* all die during our winter – are they kamikaze butterflies and why do they do it? Only the *red admiral* is said to survive our winter and then only in small numbers.

Land! I had almost survived my migration to the Scillies. Even though the rain continued to bucket down, I breathed a sigh of relief as we touched down. Someone at the Church Hall at Hugh Town has a sense of humour – the evening lecture is 'Scilly Underwater'.

It is said that the sun shines on the righteous. Incredibly, within three quarters of an hour of settling into Anchor Cottage the clouds cleared and bright sun transformed the whole scene. As I made for a small sheltered meadow where butterflies might be flying I came across two old people stuck on a stone wall where the footpath turned left. The elderly gentleman had got one leg over – the wall – but couldn't move his other one; he was stuck. His wife had climbed a small step to push him from the rear, but she had then become wedged between stones at either side, she could not go forwards because of her husband's posterior at face level; she dare not go backwards in case she fell off the step, and she could not turn. They had been locked in this slightly pornographic pose for forty minutes – looking rather like the passionate Welsh *pearl-bordered fritillaries*, but not so beautiful. I managed to lift the offending second leg over the wall and supported the old man down the steps to ground level, which then freed the trapped wife. If I hadn't wanted to walk along Holy Vail they could have been trapped in *pearl-bordered fritillary* breeding position forever. It must be frustrating getting old and not being able to get your leg over.

There were butterflies in the little meadow – *speckled woods* and *holly blues* – but nothing new. It was warm, being sheltered by a fringe of elms – yes, Scilly has escaped the ravages of Dutch Elm Disease. There were plenty of nectar-giving flowers – bluebells, red campion, whistling jacks and many more – a perfect world for butterflies.

There were grockles in the little bird hide overlooking Porthellick Lake – 'look,' one of them said to his wife, as he waved his arm out of the viewing slot – 'a moorhen'. The coot looked startled.

The sea was 'wicked', more spectacular than I had ever seen it before. Huge waves, sheets of spray, white tops and changing, moving walls of blues and greens.

A shag landed fifty yards into the swell – surf, breaking waves, high crests, low troughs worried it not at all. It was in its element.

Sarah phoned at that point, she was just going to the hairdressers; she was in her element. The gale tore at my hair – instant, natural dandruff remover – I haven't been to a hairdresser for thirty years.

I continued between the two elements, sea wave and blow wave, linked by a mobile phone; I felt slightly ashamed having a mobile phone switched on in such a place – blasphemy – courtesy of Cellnet.

How lucky shags are for not having phones.

It is easy to identify a shag – if you are another shag. If not, it is best to remember this poem by Suzanne Knowles.

> The cormorant has
> Fourteen feathers in its tail;
> Almost identical, the shag has twelve.
> One cannot fail
> To differentiate at once between
> Bird and bird sharing the sea and wind.

At one time there even used to be shag shoots on the Scillies to protect fish stocks. The conversation in two of the local pubs – *The Atlantic* and *The Mermaid* would have been interesting, 'How many shags did you have this morning?' 'Fourteen – how was it for you?' 'I only had one first thing – the other was a cormorant.'

Every so often the shag dived, it seemed to make no difference – crest of a wave or trough – it slipped under the surface easily. Even in such a surging sea the shag seemed entirely at home. Soon a guillemot landed close by. Sheltering behind a lichen-covered rock I just stood and watched this sunlit scene for far longer than it would have taken for a cut, rinse and set.

On one headland of high, whiskered rock, spray and wind were funnelled up from the sea with astonishing force. I leant into the wind – the power easily supporting my body weight. I had done this once before at Cape Point in South Africa; it would allow a butterfly to break the sound barrier. With such a gale blowing, there were no butterflies flying along the coast even with the sun shining – no **small coppers**, **common blues** or even **small tortoiseshells**. There were no **painted ladies** either and if any had come in from the sea they would have been travelling so fast their identification would have been impossible.

Tuesday May 14th

The garden of the old lighthouse on the island of St Agnes made a complete contrast to the day before – calm, sheltered, warm and secure behind a hedge of evergreen. The exotic flowers were attracting bees and butterflies, and a pair of goldfinches were pulling moss from the lawn as lining for their nest. **Holly blues** flitted around evergreen leaves and two **speckled woods** were flying in a dizzy, rotating dance. A cuckoo called clearly; what a pleasure – the authentic summer voice of the countryside still alive and well and living on the Scillies. It is not the only songbird common on the Scillies – song thrushes, blackbirds and linnets are in astonishing numbers. The thrushes and blackbirds are remarkably tame. Of course the 'experts' will maintain that the virtual lack of songbird predators on Scilly – sparrowhawks, magpies and crows has nothing to do with the booming songbird population. Presumably the favourite feast for a magpie consists of bloater paste sandwiches, followed by apricot trifle and not young song thrushes just out of the nest. It is just a coincidence that on the mainland where magpies and their friends are out of control – songbird numbers have plummeted. Perhaps too, the calling cuckoos of the sparrowhawkless Scillies show that on the mainland they too are targeted by hawks; or perhaps the magpies and crows have depleted the number of nests to host their eggs?

The garden was surrounded by evergreens to keep out the wind. On the mainland the **holly blue** butterfly normally lays its eggs on holly in the spring and ivy in the autumn – for its two generations. But on the Scillies it also breeds and feeds on the various exotic evergreens introduced as wind brakes around the gardens, and fields of bulbs and flowers.

I have never been a fan of Latin names for flowers and trees. They have seemed rather meaningless to me and so I was disappointed on asking Francis Hicks the name of the leafy shrub around his garden. He replied '*Euonymus japonica*'. 'And where does it come from?' I asked. 'Japan' was the disbelieving reply.

Like all farmers in Britain, Francis is going through a hard time. Flowers can be flown into Britain from Colombia, Malawi and South Africa, via Holland – cheaper than he can get his blooms to the mainland.

We went into his house for a cup of tea and he produced a sachet of locally produced milk – complete with a health warning: 'This milk has not been heat treated, and may therefore contain organisms harmful to health', and then came a special message for urban politicians, 'Shake to mix cream'. At least the island's milk is people milk and not kitty milk.

Friday May 17th

No time to visit the hairdresser today. With a warm haze and the promise of sun I had a problem, my beloved Butterfly Buggy was threatening to die. At the same time, fifty miles away, the **Duke of Burgundy fritillary** would be flying. There is no doubt that my faithful Daihatsu Four Trak is on its last legs; yesterday between Exeter and Bristol oily water gushed out of the engine when I stopped. Apparently after 171,000 miles a head gasket has gone, the front bumper is dented, the driver's door is bent, the headlights are stuck on main beam, there is no nearside rear indicator and the pistons are cracked. Apart from all that it is fine. Consequently I can limp along to the land of the **Duke of Burgundy** but my visit to Scotland in search of the **chequered skipper** seems in jeopardy, unless I get another car.

Another car was duly ordered at a garage in Biggleswade – yes Biggleswade – twinned with Potton as the didecoy capitals of middle England. The secret of buying a four-wheel drive vehicle in Biggleswade is to take delivery of it before the didecoys steal it.

The advice from my garage was 'go to Biggleswade', as there are so many women wanting four wheel drives in Cambridge for the 'school run' that suitable cars cost an extra £2,000 there. Why women with children at a private school need four wheel drives as their means of transport for their offspring is anybody's guess. At one time the Volvo Estate was the choice of the school-runners – the 'Volvettes'; now the choice is the Land Rover Freelander – it obviously has far more room on the dashboard for the nail file, the blusher and the Valium.

At the four-wheel drive garage – not one Daihatsu was to be seen. Apparently they last so long and are so popular among working farmers that a rival has bought them out, to phase them out. Instead, oh no, was a row of fine, polished, nearly new Freelanders, the new girlie car. In most ungirlie-like fashion I chose an olive green one in two minutes flat, without opening a door; with me shopping is not a hobby, it is an occasional necessity. To reduce its girlie image I have named the car Eric. I am sure that once introduced to buckets of cow food, baler twine and wet dogs it will get a more farm-friendly appearance.

As Eric went off to be serviced and tow-barred the Daihatsu limped off towards Whipsnade Zoo. I went with an old friend, Mick, to act as navigator and mechanic. It takes a navigator to get through the nightmare towns of Luton and Dunstable; fortunately as an ex-lorry driver he knows the short cuts to reduce the travel trauma.

I was feeling confident as we arrived at Dunstable Downs – *fritillaries* are large, bright butterflies and so it seemed just a matter of getting out of the car, finding a cowslip, the food plant of the **Duke of Burgundy**, ticking the butterfly, buying an ice cream and returning home, again avoiding, if possible, the architectural and social delights of Luton and Dunstable.

Memory is a frightening thing, locked away in the recesses of the brain are so many events and places that come tumbling out when triggered. Consequently Judgement Day must be very simple for St Peter – he plugs you into a Holy socket and all your sins and omissions are e-mailed onto the Pearly Gate website. It is a frightening thought. Fortunately for butterflies whose life-spans only stretch for days, or weeks, memory cannot be much of a factor in life or death. In a wet, cold summer they would have little to remember anyway.

From the top of the escarpment, overlooking a field full of gliders, memories come flooding back – of Sunday School outings to Whipsnade Zoo – of gliders, wallabies, elephant rides and nasty children throwing empty ice cream tubs into the ostrich enclosure. The ostriches then swallowed those cardboard containers with relish – that is enthusiasm – not gentleman's relish. How the dear little kiddies laughed as the tub-like shapes slowly sank down the long, thin necks. Even at an age of short trousers, before the arrival of acne, I was appalled. I hope St Peter's e-mailing exposé has a counter balance to list good intentions and fine thoughts.

On one such outing the charabanc actually broke down and we watched the gliders for hours – I hoped the Butterfly Buggy would not give us another memory of crunching metal and hours of waiting.

At a car park, that vaguely reminded me of butterfly location instructions, we stopped. The top of the escarpment is obviously Luton's answer to the Alps. Some very white people were trying to turn brown in the weak sun and some very fat people wearing England shirts were kicking a football about. With beer bellies and beads of sweat they epitomised the macho manliness of Blair's New Britain – vote now – think later. Behind some bushes to keep out of the wind a group of elderly people wearing coats and hats were having a picnic, they smiled without conviction. What a day – white people trying to brown and old people trying to warm.

Once going down-hill we kept warm; we were soon away from people too. It is amazing how most urban trippers into the countryside will not wander more than 200 yards from a car park. I suppose it is fear of the unknown; strange farm animals, rustics with rural accents and bird and animal droppings – surely a health hazard. Perhaps the whole countryside should be hoovered twice weekly to remove all hazardous waste. It could then be stored and processed in Parliament Square – perhaps it is already.

Rabbits had grazed the grass low but had managed to avoid eating some of the cowslips. But where were these large, distinctive *fritillaries*? There were **brimstones**, **tortoiseshells**, and the ever present **cabbage white** but the aristocratic **Duke of Burgundy** obviously had no intention of mixing with commoners. Risking life and limb over nettle-covered rabbit holes we struggled to some rough grass inside the glider field. Mick's feet and ankles were stung and scratched – wearing flip-flops he had obviously been talking to Sarah about the footwear needed for butterfly hunting. Only too late did he realise that a butterfly safari needs the same clothing as an elephant safari; the only real difference, as the **Duke of Burgundy fritillary** was demonstrating, is that butterflies are much harder to see than elephants.

There were no **Duke of Burgundies** in the rough grass – but there was a **green hairstreak**. It was such a beautiful little butterfly I did pause to exchange pleasantries. 'Good morning little green butterfly.' Oh dear – talking to butterflies now – where will it all end. We puffed and panted back to the top of the steep escarpment – Mick's flip-flops were better on short grass than rabbit holes.

The car park and 'down' is owned by the National Trust. As you leave your car in the car park to descend the escarpment, the front of the nearby building looks like a picnic palace for crisps and ice cream. As you return, gasping and wheezing, via the back of the building you read: 'Countryside Centre'. What a cunning plan – sell ice creams first and the countryside second.

A kind lady explained that we were in the wrong place. Oh no – all that suffering for rabbits and **brimstones**; we had to be in the car park 'overlooking the bison'. 'You are the second people to be looking for the **Duke of Burgundy fritillary** today.'

At the bison enclosure – the bison looked distinctly bored. I wonder if bison ever think 'butterflies'; if they don't they will be similar to most of the people in Britain. Fortunately in the car park there was a woman who clearly meant business; not for her the football shirt and sun bathing – she was wearing safari suit khaki and applying generous dollops of suntan lotion to her arms. She confirmed that we were in the right area for this fluttering aerial aristocrat, and as we left the Butterfly Buggy behind we were confident of success. With cowslips galore, a steep, south-facing slope and cleared brambles the site seemed perfect – the only worry was the weather – the sun had become hazy and the clouds in the west were beginning to build.

But where was this big, beautiful butterfly? At times I felt like a pheasant shoot beater – walking high and low – but the only wings were yellow and *tortoiseshell* and I really was not interested in magpies. Suddenly a welcome call came – 'Oi' – and Mick waved me downwards – to the lowest point, where safari woman had arrived. Then came a simple lesson – before setting out on a butterfly safari, find out what your butterfly looks like. There, at the bottom of a little, sheltered dip was not a large flamboyant butterfly – but a small dingy butterfly, almost moth-like when it flew. Yes, it was the butterfly with the name '***Duke of Burgundy fritillary***'; the most important feature of the butterfly is that it is not a ***fritillary*** and so its grand name in no way reflects the character of the insect. Perhaps it reflects the real Duke of Burgundy's sense of humour – who knows. The actual butterfly resembles a ***skipper*** – a cross between a ***dingy*** and a ***grizzled***; perhaps 'gringy' or 'drizzled skipper' would have been a more appropriate name.

It settled, wings open, before seeing off a ***brimstone***, an ***orange tip*** and a ***large white*** – his lordship was evidently very aggressive with butterflies twice and three times his size. I was pleased to see this little butterfly – not just for the tick – but for itself. The ***Duke of Burgundy*** is in decline because of the intensification of agriculture, tree felling, hedge removal and lack of interest. It is only a small butterfly – but if we can't be bothered to safeguard the small, will our indifference eventually rebound against ourselves? If we won't look after nature – why should nature look after us?

Saturday May 18th

What will I see today? I am going to Yorkshire – between Barnsley and Huddersfield – for a Countryside Restoration Trust Open Day. It sounds a dreadful place – but in fact Margaret Wood is a very attractive place; thirty acres of beauty and tranquillity on a south-facing valley side near the village of Upper Denby. It was bought and renamed by a Gritty Yorkshireman, Duncan Elliot, in memory of his wife and he in turn left it to the CRT.

It is our only Northern property so far. A local – Edward Nobe looks after it for the CRT. His big claim to fame – living almost in the exact middle of Britain – is that he is a volunteer lifeboat man. He is the most landlocked lifeboat man possible – being over 1,000 feet above sea level with a journey of 70 miles just to reach the sea. Whenever there is an emergency he usually arrives in time to help take the lifeboat out of the sea on its return to land. For

the sake of Edward's car it would help if all sea captains would run aground, or get wrecked slowly.

I sped up to Denby Dale in the car of Ken, the CRT's treasurer. It was a frightening experience; he has a butterfly mind and as his conversation jumps from subject to subject, so do his eyes. While he was driving it would have helped if he had looked at the road and the speedometer now and again.

Yorkshire was bathed in drizzle and mist, but through it, Margaret Wood and its bluebells looked beautiful, a picture of blue and green mistiness – an artist's wash – still and silent, apart from birdsong and the dripping of water from the bursting canopy of leaves. On this morning, at this time, there was an ethereal quality – almost spiritual – not me talking to trees – but the trees talking to me in a very ancient and deep-rooted language.

As water dripped, the small stream murmured over rocks and droplets hung from the bluebell flower heads. Not even a ***drizzled skipper*** would have flown in this dampness. I must visit Margaret Wood again in sunlight to see what butter-flies are attracted to its leaves and dappled light – to its glades and shades. Even so in such a place at such a season, something was missing – not a butterfly, but a bird's song, the call of the cuckoo – its silence bellowed – but who hears or cares?

Sunday May 19th

The sun and summer have returned. The Great British Butterfly Safari has already taught me a huge amount – one thing is simple – although I actively look for butterflies along our hedges in high summer – at this time of year I don't – I notice flowers, birds and blossom but I don't search for butterflies along our numerous hedgerows and through our chunks of shrub and scrub. But it seems perfect for the **green hairstreak** – the food plants are there already; dogwood, blackthorn, bramble and bird's foot trefoil and we have good quantities of all four.

My old late father was buried at the foot of a hedge. That is where he wanted to go – free and uncrowded – so that is where he went. I want to go into another hedge – I don't like crowds either. My old lurcher, Bramble, is already there and I want to go next to him. It is a wonderful hedge containing hawthorn, ash, crab apple, buckthorn, elder, dogwood, wild roses, spindle and blackthorn, and there are blackberries, hops and strings of bryony when the hedgerow harvest is at its height. With such a mixture of light and shade, flower and blossom, leaf and thorn it is the perfect place for the **green hairstreak** – that is perfect through my eyes, which are not butterfly eyes – or does the butterfly decide through its feet?

This is not as idiotic as it seems – because some butterflies taste with their feet. They actually check the food plant through their feet – we can taste feet – at least some ex-politician once delighted in sucking toes – but butterflies taste with their feet. On the Scillies I watched a **red admiral** for a full five minutes – just shifting its feet on a nettle leaf; was it tasting it? The nettle is its main food plant – once it has arrived as a caterpillar. They can smell too of course – but not through their feet; do the feet of butterflies smell however? Life is so full of challenge and mystery.

There was little mystery along the hedgerow. Alas I could find no **green hairstreak** – just a larger, slower **speckled wood** – for once not flying in ever decreasing circles. The females live much more leisurely lives than the males – spending their time basking in the sun or feeding on aphid honeydew in the tree canopy, while the males patrol and display. It sounds as if *Homo sapiens* has quite a lot in common with butterflies after all.

Monday May 20th

Dust to dust; ashes to ashes – Eric has today replaced the beloved Butterfly Buggy. To acclimatise, Sarah drove me to a funeral. I left late; we arrived early – I can see why it has become a girly car; the way she drove it almost became my funeral too. The dashboard does have plenty of room for Valium.

Tuesday May 21st – Lark Rise

A group of bird-watchers is visiting the Trust land today – at 7.30pm – just when bird activity slows down. If the sun is out there will be a few goodnight whistles and warbles and that will be that.

Butterflies too will be shutting down for the night. After a day of flopping and flying here and there they will be having the equivalent of a cup of cocoa before becoming nocturnally comatose. I often feel nocturnally comatose before writing my butterfly diary – I do not find a leaf, dark corner, or grass clump to shelter under; I simply collapse on the bed or in the armchair and I am asleep within minutes – almost seconds. I would make a good butterfly because of the speed with which I can change from fully conscious to comatose – unconscious. I have to confess too that I don't just settle for evening or night only; I can sleep anywhere at any time – just like a butterfly, just slightly noisier and not quite so beautiful.

It was a butterfly day all day until early evening. Should I go and look for a **brown argus** or should I wait for the evening? I waited for the evening.

At six the sun could barely shine through high thin cloud. At seven the sun had entirely vanished behind the low thick cloud. At 7.30 as the bird-watchers began to assemble it drizzled – at 7.45 as we walked into the first field – stair rods – the rain fell by the bucketful.

Some of the birdie people wore weatherproofs and wellington boots – some wore jumpers and shoes more suited to shopping – it was grey, wet and dripping; some of them were grey, wet and dripping. A barn owl flew by the hedge – to take shelter 200 yards along; it was almost certainly a sign that the barn owls are breeding in a nearby nest box for the second year running.

We abandoned the walk at half way. The sodden ground had soaked my jeans and the water had percolated downwards into my wellies – with no bus or underground train to catch in the rain, Sarah had given the walk a miss – **brown argus**, sunken argus, drowned argus, or no argus at all – she did not want to join the grey and the wet.

Back at the farmyard the bird-watchers were able to see another bird. While we had been walking through the rain – a fox had been sneaking up in the wet and killed the oldest goose – leaving the rest of the geese apparently traumatised. The body of the old goose lay spread-eagled in a spray of blood and feathers – the fox could have been a disciple of Damian Hirst – perhaps we should preserve the scene and enter it for this year's Turner Prize; I'm sure if the piece was described as rare and signed by Reynard Vulpes or Julian Fox, the London art establishment and the BBC would hail it as an artistic triumph. To sum up their grasp of country life it could be called 'Dead Duck' – they wouldn't know the difference, and, in any case the word 'goose' would excite them too much. Not many of the bird-watchers wanted to see the dead bird.

Sarah came to see the goose; it made her angry, 'bloody fox' – reality. The old gander had spent years with his now dead mate and each night for years they had shared a small shed together.

As the murkiness moved towards darkness he again wandered into his shed, this time alone. Geese have such expressive faces; his seemed to be full of grief; a picture of a grief-stricken gander – no Turner Prize material there.

Incredibly one of his daughters – with no persuasion – followed him into the shed and sat next to him – waiting for Rachael, my younger sister, to shut them

in. It was touching – moving – astonishing – do birds or butterflies know more than we think they know – do they understand grief?

We checked the hens – free-range – and shut in at dusk, they were ten short – out of fifty. It seems as if the fox has visited before – in daylight – the hens have vanished – perhaps the goose was too heavy to carry away?

Sarah was astonished –

'What are the hens doing?' she asked.

'Perching.'

'Why?'

'That's what they do at night.'

'It looks very uncomfortable.'

'It would be for you – but you are not a hen.'

The rain fell; the goose was dead; the butterflies were comatose; Sarah was amazed; I was cold – another happy day in Bumpkinland was over.

Thursday May 23rd – to Scotland

I have been phoning Scotland. The **chequered skipper** should be flying – I should be going to Scotland but the **chequered skipper** is not flying – it is sheltering – it keeps raining, it needs an umbrella. It is raining here too – but I will take a risk and go to Scotland anyway – to a rather unusual birthday party.

I hope it stops raining – I have waited to see the **chequered skipper** for years; ever since I first met Miriam Rothschild. At one time she had the **chequered skipper** on her estate and it was common in many parts of the country. But gradually the butterfly was lost until now; the only *Chequered Skipper* in England is the village pub in Miriam's little village of Ashton Wold in Northamptonshire – *The Chequered Skipper*. Why the butterfly has disappeared from all its old English haunts is not fully understood; nor is it understood why it is now a Scottish butterfly – with its main stronghold being a remote area near Fort William.

As Eric pounded up the motorway and into the Highlands things were not promising – the clouds got thicker and wetter and the rain sluiced down. Sarah was looking quite exotic for this hunt with scarlet toenails and blue eyelashes; in butterfly terms she was more of a **painted lady** than a **dingy skipper**. Before setting out I was told that all I needed was twenty minutes of warm sun and the butterfly would fly – from behind over-worked windscreen wipers twenty minutes of warm sun seemed as unlikely as a coconut palm in an igloo.

Country living is clearly beginning to damage Sarah's health; she too has started talking to strange things – perhaps trees, bees, and beautiful scenes should carry a government health warning.

'Hallo tree.'

'Hallo church.'

'Hallo pretty village.'

'Hallo wonderful cows.'

'Hallo river.'

'Hallo butterfly.'

When Prince Charles confessed to talking to trees – the downmarket media questioned his sanity. Sarah is talking to everything – but why not? After the confession of Prince Charles, David Bellamy admitted that he actually hugged trees. For the sake of solidarity I went one better. I kissed a tree – fortunately its bark was softer than its bite.

At the end of a winding road a wide valley opened up in front of us – mountains, fields, forests and fast-flowing streams. This was too much for Sarah – her blue eyelashes widened.

'Hallo everything!' she exclaimed in wonder.

It was inspired – she should be a writer of pop songs, for as she said 'Hallo everything', from the fifth playing of Eric's Simon and Garfunkel tape – they sang 'Hallo lamp post'.

Talk to trees and valleys – you are mad. Talk to lamp posts – you are international super-stars.

> *Hallo lamp post what you knowing*
> *I've come to watch your flowers a growing.*

Oh dear – talking to lamp posts and watching flowers a-growing – who is mad?

Not liking the competition Sarah wanted something different; 'Can't we listen to something local?' That was easy – a press of a button and a voice speaking in Gaelic emerged.

'Not as local as that.'

Next came a Scottish disc jockey – isn't it odd how Scottish accents sound

familiar in England, not only with a majority of disc jockeys, but also MPs, Union leaders and government spokesmen. Scotland doesn't need independence – it already rules Britain.

As we crossed Rannoch Moor even the rain looked spectacular – it was raining cats and dogs. Visit Scotland and see rain – vertical rain, horizontal rain, swirling rain and several types of drizzle. Rocks, heather, lochans, mountain, moorland, wilderness, that is Rannoch Moor. It is a place where the heart and spirit feel free – there are ancient sounds and moods that still stir feelings deep within us. They link us to our distant roots – roots within nature – not new shoots that try to dominate and by-pass nature.

In that wilderness are some of our rarest breeding birds – including divers – in all that rain, most appropriate.

The West Coast of Scotland is spectacular – cliffs and castles, bays and beaches, islands and inlets. It is far too good for the urban Scots who make up the Scottish Parliament. It is 'Camper-Van-Land' with every lay-by, nook and cranny filled with English camper vans. Rain can be watched so much more cheaply from a camper van than from a hotel lounge.

At the edge of Loch Creagon, I stopped to look for the Glasdrum Nature Reserve. Butterfly directions all sound the same; 'then you reach a T junction – go left for a mile and a half, then you see a gate by a tree and a sign where you can park your car. Go over the stile and follow the path'. There is always a gate without a tree, a park without a sign and stile without a path.

The reserve is said to be one of the last refuges of the ***chequered skipper***. As I looked at two gates – the sun came out –'am I going to be lucky?' As I pondered, a camper van drove up and stopped. The driver had lost his tri-coloured terrier 'Patch'. It had gone missing twenty miles away, the week before. If we should see it; 'Would you phone me on my mobile?' It was, it seemed to me, a forlorn hope – I have never seen or found a 'lost' dog yet.

It was a forlorn hope looking for the ***chequered skipper***. Despite late sun it was too cold; plenty of bugs, beetles and daddy-long-legs (please excuse the scientific name) and moths, but no butterflies.

We gave up and slid and slud (sliding through mud) down the mountainside to walk back to the parked up Eric, along the loch shore. Good Heavens! Approaching from the other direction was a tri-coloured terrier. 'Patch. Patch – come here – good boy,' I shouted. Patch was a girl and made off up the hillside. We rushed through brambles and flowering gorse to get to the car – the vivid yellow flowers clashing badly with Sarah's blue eyelashes.

There was a camper van on the other side of the loch – I raced Eric there. It was like Formula One – round a roundabout the wrong way and burning tyres. 'Quick! Patch is by the other shore,' I screamed. The driver looked at me as if I was insane – it was the wrong camper van.

Oh dear, the mobile phone wouldn't work, not even for 999. At last a ringing tone and I gave directions. We sped off to the rendezvous – Eric roaring, and soon the camper van arrived. A door was flung open, and there in all her glory was 'Patch' – once again with her owners after a week of wandering and anxiety. We hadn't seen a **chequered skipper** but we had reunited a happy couple with their best friend. Sarah's blue eyelashes fluttered with emotion; 'Call this The Great British Butterfly Safari?' she said, 'it's been more like an episode of Lassie!'

With that it started to rain cats and dogs again.

Friday May 24th – Scotland

Here comes the sun. I can feel a song coming on. Here comes the cloud – I don't think I will sing. Cuil Bay looked wonderful – one day I will have to come back, with a camper van.

'Then you reach a T junction – go left for a mile and a half, then you see a gate by a tree and a sign where you can park your car. Go over the stile and follow the path.'

We found a gate without a tree and a park without a sign and a stile without a path, and as the sun came out in acres of blue sky we battled upwards. Sarah longed to be in Hammersmith with escalators – so did I. We trudged upwards through bramble, gorse, bracken and birch – to overhead power cables. Yes, *chequered skippers* love electricity – or at least the vegetation beneath the power lines – it is periodically hacked away to keep the cables clear – creating scrub – not woodland, thicket or forest – but stunted scrub of birch, sallow, oak and bracken.

Yesterday the sun's evening angle carried little heat; today coming in from the east it was a sun trap – warm, soft and soothing.

There were butterflies; a *fritillary* – which one? Almost certainly a *pearl-bordered*: there were *brimstones*, *small tortoiseshells*, and what's that moth warming its open wings on bracken? It's … it's … it's not a moth, it's a butterfly – it's a *chequered skipper*. I hugged Sarah in triumph; she pirouetted in delight. There was another settled on the bright blue flowers of bugle – the same colour as Sarah's eye lashes – the lucky butterfly eyelashes.

What a beautiful little butterfly – the *chequered skipper* – what a pleasure meeting it in such a place. Yellow spots on chocolate wings – wings that fly fast and aggressively at other butterflies – but at rest they open to absorb the sun. The *chequered skipper* disappeared in England in 1975 – 177 years after it had been found in Bedfordshire. I hope the Scottish *skippers* face a better future up there among the birch and bugle. Warm drizzle breezed in – and still the *skippers* flew. We didn't trudge back to Eric – we almost skipped – skipped for the *chequered skipper* – it seemed the right thing to do.

Saturday May 25th

It's party time – for who or for what? It had been a spectacular journey to get here – past Ben Nevis and its magnificent neighbours – along valleys – past forests and lochs, moors and mountains. If there weren't so many battles to be fought further south I could come and live up here – drop out – hide away –

think – write poetry – walk the dog – read books – cut logs – search for butter-flies – it would be real life reclaimed.

Real life reclaimed – what a wish. Instead I have come to a party – a party for what? We stopped at a little stone bungalow perched on a valley side below the Cairngorm Mountains – still streaked with snow. People were already gathering. 'Happy Birthday to you, happy birthday to you, happy birthday dear … reindeer … REINDEER! Happy birthday to you.'

Yes, it is a celebration to mark the fiftieth anniversary of the return of the reindeer to Scotland. Legend has it that over 1,000 years ago the Vikings hunted reindeer to extinction in Caithness – county boundaries in Scotland 1,000 years ago – incredible. History suggests that reindeer died out in Scotland between 2–3,000 years ago because of climatic change or over-hunting.

Whatever happened, a little Laplander called Michel Utsi, and a tall American, Dr Ethel Lindgren, saw the Cairngorms, the Caledonian pines, the reindeer moss – and thought 'reindeer'. Fifty years ago they brought their reindeer into Scotland from Sweden and here we were singing 'Happy Birthday' to reindeer. They were a remarkable couple – little and large – short and tall – high and low. How did they kiss – how did they do all sorts of things? The most inaccurate assumption is 'everybody is the same height lying down'; no they are not.

Did love and affection involve platform shoes, standing on boxes, or ropes and pulleys? We will never know. All we do know is that the reindeer have done well – they have multiplied without the use of platform hooves, ropes and pulleys –

and without the present reindeer keepers Alan and Tilly Smith taking them to family planning or udder-feeding clinics. Alan and Tilly are fine people who had invited all those with links to the reindeer over fifty years to a party.

The rain came; the temperature plummeted and we went to wish the reindeer happy birthday on the hill. Alan, Tilly and the reindeer were happy in their natural element – I slowly froze – Sarah's nose turned red and her blue eyelashes ran – giving her the appearance of an Apache Squaw.

To have compared Sarah's nose with Rudolph the Red Nosed Reindeer's would have been unfair. Reindeer do not have red noses – they have warm, soft, dry, velvet noses, which we could touch. So incredible are the noses of reindeer that I have written a book about them – *Why the Reindeer has a Velvet Nose*. It is the definitive, scientific work on the Reindeer's nose – based entirely on fantasy: consequently it should have a ready market in political circles. I have dedicated it to Sarah as a guide to nose colour and to compensate her for all the dangers and discomfort of The Great British Butterfly Safari.

In the afternoon the sun came out and we walked in warmth through the ancient pines and heather where the early reindeer lived. Some reindeer came with us – it was a wonderful walk and the afternoon heat made such a contrast to the morning.

In the evening it was Ceilidh time – eat, drink and be happy. The band was extraordinary – three dour, unsmiling musicians. They could play their instruments, but they had very short necks – we called them the 'No Neck Band'. I expect it comes from the Scottish habit of tossing the caber. The impact of the arms jerking the caber upwards, compacts the head into the shoulders making the neck disappear completely. It was a good party and the No Neck Band played until we dropped. Sarah's nose had gone from red to white and her cheeks had gone from white to red.

'You've caught the sun,' I said.

'I haven't – it's blusher,' she said.

I wonder what had turned the band's hair ginger.

Wednesday May 29th

Telegraph Field is the first field the Countryside Restoration Trust bought in July 1993 – twenty acres of wildlife-dead, wall-to-wall wheat – right up to the brook-edge. We called it Telegraph Field because along its southern side are five dishes in a row – part of Cambridge University's 'Radio Telescope'. In addition when the CRT was launched it was readers of *The Daily Telegraph* who first dipped their hands into their pockets to help us buy 'Telegraph' field.

Now there are traditional hay meadows across the flood plain, to the brook-edge, grown from a Miriam Rothschild meadow mixture of seventy species of grasses and wildflowers. The hay meadow is divided from the arable by a long hedge of fourteen types of tree and shrub and there is a grass margin – a grass strip around the whole area of cultivation.

Birds and butterflies have found the hay meadow and the grassy strips. A hare got up from almost under our feet and Sarah jumped – hares are apparently rare – not here they are not.

The **brown argus** butterfly has found the field – a beautiful small brown butterfly – being brown it is a member of the 'blue family'. I wanted to see a **brown argus** – but Sarah's lucky eyelashes had reverted to black.

There were **small tortoiseshells**, a **peacock**, **whites** and still a few **orange tips** – skylarks sang and the laughing call of green woodpeckers came from across the wood. The breeze was incredible, almost edible – warm and nectar filled – a cocktail of scents – a butterfly's delight – red clover, ox-eye daisy, elder flowers, crab apple blossom and 'may' – rich, sweet-scented and 'is there honey still for tea'.

Honey bees have all but disappeared but bumble bees were travelling from flower to flower. No **brown argus** – but a field full of life – brought back to life.

Friday May 31st

The weather is not being helpful. The sun appears; it goes; the temperature drops; it rains; it stops; the wind blows – there are butterflies to see – **blues-fritillaries** – and the **brown** that is a **blue**. There is the **swallowtail** to see – arguably Britain's most striking butterfly with a wingspan of nearly four inches.

The weather forecast is blue sky – with showers – the **swallowtail**, although only found in the Fens likes neither wind nor water – at least water in the form of raindrops. I must risk it or else I will get a butterfly-jam.

Hickling Broad is low-lying marshland – not far from the Norfolk coast. The 'Broad' is a large stretch of water – flooded peat diggings from the 14th Century – dug when the locals wanted fuel – not roses.

Out of the wind it was warm; in the wind there was an edge to it. When the sun appeared it was bright – but fluffy, speeding cloud brought shadow. The warden was not too hopeful. 'You might be lucky – but it's a bit early – they like the sun; they don't like cold wind like this morning.'

Can I believe it? Sarah is wearing wellington boots – the first pair she has ever owned in her life – there is not much call for them in Hammersmith High Street. There is not much call for shag-me boots at Hickling Broad – although there must be some doubt about the rest of Norfolk. The blue eyelashes were back – two damsel flies of an almost identical hue, flew up to have a closer look – 'can I? can't I? – shall I? shan't I?' They couldn't and they didn't.

The *swallowtail* needs plants of bog and fen in order to breed successfully with the favourite food plants being milk parsley, angelica, wild carrot and fennel – quite a herb-rich salad. For nectar the butterflies like thistles, ragged robin and the flowers of milk parsley.

The *swallowtail* is slow flying – but nothing could be slow flying in this wind – a butterfly black, gold, blue, red – climbing, travelling, vanishing, directly over Sarah's head. She tried to follow its line of flight – but gave up, clinging to the handrail. She would have toppled over backwards into the water if she had kept watching, flat on her back with her eyelashes breaking the surface like two bright blue damsel flies. 'Was it a *swallowtail*?' I asked hopefully. 'I didn't see it,' replied my adjudicator. Oh dear, it could be the difference between success and failure.

If I had been a *swallowtail* I would have not bothered in this wind. A party of Dutchmen passed us looking at every plant, feather and wingbeat through their binoculars. It was a good job they did. At a bend in the path one of them nudged me, 'Look there a little – a-svollotails'. His English was better than my Dutch, and there, on a sheltered bend of phragmites (a reed) was a newly emerged *swallowtail* with its wings open. One svollo doesn't make a summer – but one svollotail definitely helps to make a Butterfly Safari.

June

Saturday June 1st

Cricket is one of the great joys of an English summer. Not the great green bush cricket, the mole cricket or the wood cricket – but cricket – bat against ball – willow on leather – cucumber sandwiches with a pint of bitter. Not much will make me miss a game – as with every passing season I become increasingly aware that the end of my career in village cricket is drawing ever closer. But again, this year, I am missing a game to attend Miriam Rothschild's summer party. In an age when ordinariness is praised as a virtue – unashamedly I still have heroes. I admire people who are not ordinary – who have achieved things – and who, ignoring their own egos, have done things because they believed that they needed doing. That immediately rules out virtually every ego-polishing incumbent of the House of Commons.

Miriam Rothschild is one of my greatest heroes – even a heroine – self-taught, conservation-driven, with a world vision. Her parties are to get conservationists – to meet and eat, think and drink and to co-operate to spread the conservation message. It needs spreading.

I reach Miriam by trundling along the A14. I turn right at an architectural eye-sore (lie back and shut your eyes – think of a building – obtrusive, out of keeping with the landscape, not made out of local materials, lacking in line, too angular, too big, too ugly and too alien – out of time, place and scale) that is where I leave the A14 – to drive to Miriam's.

I arrive at Miriam's where I see architectural inspiration (unobtrusive, in keeping with the landscape, made out of local materials, built with skill, craftsmanship and pride – in place, in scale and attractive) the village of Ashton Wold, near Oundle.

Past the village green – surrounded by thatched cottages made out of local stone. Once, after a cottage had been re-thatched with Norfolk reed during the winter – a *swallowtail* butterfly appeared in the middle of an Ashton Wold summer – much to the surprise of both Miriam and the *swallowtail* butterfly.

Past *The Chequered Skipper* pub – feeling smug, at last I have seen the real thing, not just the pub sign; up a rutted roadway to the big house – almost hidden in trees – a new village, Victorian-style – dreamed, designed and created by Miriam's father. He had money – the village was driven by vision. Most of today's 'new' villages are driven only by the vision of money.

Miriam is a living legend – a conservation legend – it was so novel to go to the front door of a living legend and find it open. Nigel was visibly shaken. Miriam at 94 was on her electronic buggy – she has been almost as important to me in my butterfly education as Gordon Beningfield – one the scientist and the other the artist – both loving butterflies. Miriam's loves were butterflies and fleas. I told her of my dash to Scotland for my first encounter with a real **chequered skipper**.

Sarah felt too intimidated to meet the great butterfly Dame – it would have made an extraordinary meeting – the 94-year-old and the 23-year-old. Would a modern Miriam go watching butterflies with blue-painted eye lashes while listening to 'Vibe FM'? She certainly had spirit in her youth – playing women's cricket for England under an assumed name so that her father did not find out. She still loves sport and her favourite television channels are Sky Sports 1, 2 and 3.

We mingled, chatted and exchanged views – there were people who specialised in trees, grasses, birds and butterflies: regeneration, conservation and restoration. Lunch is usually long – and the overspill is the garden – each year the visitors go off to see butterflies, or dragonflies, or hay meadows or scrub. At 94, Miriam still has dreams, projects and hopes – this year she wants to interest the lunchers in bats – she wants them to stay on until dusk to view bats over the lake – pipistrelle and long–eared – not cricket.

We could not stay as we had an appointment in the afternoon – if the sun shone – and it shone. We had an appointment with **wood white** butterflies in Salcey Forest – sadly a sunny afternoon could not be spent waiting for bats. I had hoped to go to Herefordshire to see the **wood white** – but the weather intervened. Instead with the sun out – this opportunity had to be taken.

The **wood white** is the rarest British white and it is getting rarer as woodland is cleared – or not managed. It favours woodland rides and clearings and only flies in sunlight, it is not easy flying in sunlight in a wood. Salcey Forest is an ancient wood, criss-crossed with rides and bridleways. With a pincer movement of expanding urban sprawl advancing on two sides from Milton Keynes and Northampton, plus the noise and pollution of the nearby M1 – how much longer can Salcey Forest keep its **wood whites**, or even remain a forest?

We quickly found them – along a track – with trimmed-up scrub on one side and tangle of leaves and branches on the other. What delicate butterflies with a languid, floating flight – and gently shaded underwings when the wings come together. The feeding butterfly has closed wings; and again the caterpillar would never eat a cabbage – the wild pea family – yes, the tame cabbage family – no. The male flies whenever the sun shines; up, down, along, over, under – never still – patrolling, repelling, searching, attracting. With his close-up lens in place Nigel did the same – up, down, over, under, stumble, fumble, curse – 'where's it gone?'

Patience is more than a virtue when natural butterfly photography is attempted. Many modern-day photographers simply catch their subject in a net, place it in a container and put it in the fridge until it becomes cold and comatose. Then, open the fridge, open the container, stick the butterfly on its food plant or nectar plant, let it warm up slowly – wings open, click, click, click – one de-frosted photographed butterfly. The motto of some butterfly photographers ought to be: *cooling is fooling; heating is cheating* – but it is not.

On this butterfly safari there has been no cheating and there will be no cheating. Today it has been the **wood white** – number twenty-two. How many to go, I do not know and dare not think.

Sunday June 2nd

More sun and no wind. Will the **brown argus** be flying in Telegraph Field today? **Common blues** were everywhere – and little brown butterflies with open wings and orange dots along the edges – there must have been at least a dozen of them. 'Sarah is that the **brown argus** – or a female **common blue**?'

'How should I know? You tell me, you're the expert.'

'How should I know? You're the adjudicator.'

We were the two unknowing, standing in scent and flowers – seeing butterflies and not recognising what we were looking at. Why can butterflies be so difficult – why do female **common blues** not look like male **common blues**? I hope that a female **brown argus** can recognise a male **brown argus**!

Monday June 3rd

When in doubt call Trevor. Same place, same sun, same time, same scent, same flowers – no butterflies. Where are they? Where have they gone? 'Honest Trevor, they were here yesterday. It's just a couple of degrees cooler, and twelve brown butterflies fewer.' We searched – stopped – stared – hoped. There were odd bumble bees, then a '*blue*' but not a brown '*blue*' – why call a family of butterflies '*blues*' if one is not at all blue?

The food plants of the **brown argus** are the rock rose and the common storksbill – neither are common – if they occur at all – in the hay meadow. Trevor has a theory that they have also started to use red clover – that is why the once uncommon **brown argus** is becoming the more common **brown argus**.

Then at last: a beautiful small brown butterfly with chocolate wings fringed with white and a band of orange spots. 'It's a **brown argus**,' Trevor judged with confidence, 'the dark females of the **common blue** always have a tinge of blue – the **brown argus** hasn't the slightest hint of blue.' Number twenty-three.

Tuesday June 4th

No butterflies today – but bees – or more accurately bee orchids. Four of them in perfect condition in our little farm field where we first sowed Miriam's magic meadow mix twelve years ago. The bee orchids come and go – flowers of mystery and mimicry. From a distance, they look so much like bumble bees that even amorous bumble bees can't tell the difference. The questions are – who copied who and how did they do it? Sarah asked me if she could pick one – I told her that she had more chance of winning the Eurovision Song Contest.

I am panicking – a telephone call to the Isle of Wight reveals that the **Glanville fritillary** was flying earlier than usual this year because of the warm spring, and its flying time is nearly over. If I don't get into Eric soon and head south – it will be finished – two or three weeks earlier than usual.

The **Glanville fritillary** is our rarest **fritillary** – only to be found in any numbers on the Isle of Wight. If I miss it now – I will miss it completely and there is nowhere else to see it. What is worse, there is only one generation a year.

What a strange butterfly – on the very southern, crumbling edge of Britain – almost falling into the sea – the butterfly is also on the northern most edge of its European range – a butterfly quite literally on the edge – the butterfly edge of Britain.

The weather forecast sent me into greater panic – tomorrow the early morning will be fine – with heavy rain coming in from the south; the afternoon will be awash. Oh dear – it will be a race against time – a rush against rain – but where will we find the **Glanville fritillary** on the Isle of Wight?

Fortunately I have several contacts on the Island. The first was out –

apparently business is booming – he is one of the Island's undertakers. All the other advice was contradictory. The first said 'go there' – the second 'no, don't go there, *Glanvilles* haven't been seen there for some time – go here'. The third: 'who on earth told you that? – No don't go here – *Glanvilles* haven't been doing well here – go up there'. Help – what do I do? – butterfly minds and butterfly directions are not easy to follow – there, here, up there – it all sounds very hit and miss.

Computers are apparently helpful in times of crisis – if you know how to switch them on. Sarah switched mine on – and soon like a pianist she was tapping out maps in colour – near and far – covering the Isle of Wight – remarkable. The close-ups were in such fine detail that the only things missing were the butterflies themselves.

> Isle of Wight here we come.
> *Glanville fritillary* here we come.
> Cold Front – here it comes.
> It's the race against rain!

Wednesday June 5th

5.30am Early morning – blue-blue-blue-blue in every direction, not a cloud in the sky. Blue in the passenger seat too – Sarah is fluttering her blue eyelashes – we can't go wrong. I was feeling confident.

'What's brown, steaming and comes out of Cowes?

Quite rightly, Sarah ignored me. 'A steamer from the Isle of Wight.' They don't have steamers any more – and we are going to Fishbourne, not coming from Cowes – but who cares on a morning like this?

7.30am Traffic flow south is good – weather flow north – slightly worrying. Basingstoke in sunlight. I never, ever thought I would be pleased to see it – but there it was, looking wonderful; to the south it is not promising and the horizon shows a black line of cloud.

8.30am Portsmouth – the worst is happening – we are in hazy cloud – there is weak sunlight but southwards the cloud gets thicker.

The ferry is surprisingly large – I like island ferries. A ferry turns a journey into an adventure and it limits the number of people, cars and lorries that can get onto an island. I hope the Isle of Wight is never joined to the mainland by a bridge – it will remove some of its character and swamp it with visitors.

It was a clean, recently painted ferry with a change of colour just above the water line – I assume that is the Plimsoll Line – the line which if it sinks below the water signifies that the boat is overloaded. It was named after Samuel Plimsoll who campaigned for social justice and fair working conditions for seamen. He got elected into Parliament – but stood down of his own accord – he was disillusioned – even in the 1880s there were too many egos and vested interests – Oh what a surprise. I wish the House of Commons would have its own Plimsoll Line today to measure the weight of egos and vested interests – it would sink without trace.

It takes half an hour to cross the Solent. It took half an hour for the hazy sunlight to turn to cloud – we were running out of time – so Sarah drove. It made no difference – her girl-racer instincts were of no use – once behind a bus on the Isle of Wight – the winding narrow roads mean that you stay behind a bus.

Wednesday in June on the Isle of Wight appears to be 'Pensioner Picnic Day' or 'Saga Circular Tours'. Bespectacled old ladies seemed to be glaring or staring out of every window; the tripper buses must have special racks for zimmer frames, walking sticks and handbags.

We stopped close to St Catherine's Point. The sea was a sheet of grey – the cloud was a sheet of grey – which gradually turned thicker and darker and it was coming our way.

We walked to the side of the lighthouse – looking for 'undercliff'. The **Glanville fritillary** really does favour land full of cracks, movement and slips, where the clays, sandstones and shales are sliding and crumbling into the sea. The small cliffs looked perfect – but where would the butterflies be? Where clay had become watery ooze – moving downwards and seawards, I chose my steps carefully – picking out solid from the bog. Oh dear – pavements in Hammersmith are smooth, uniform and stable – they have no bog. I skipped across – Sarah – stepped – sank – staggered – and stopped. Her sports shoes had disappeared in thick, squelching bog – with her feet inside them; her black trousers would now have their very own Plimsoll Line. I pulled her and she struggled to the side – leaving one sports shoe behind. I dug it out with my stick before helping her hobble, with one shoe on and one shoe off – to the edge of the sea. She washed her feet and trousers – the water was cold – I washed her shoes. 'Why did it do that?' she asked. 'Why are they doing that?' I asked – her feet and hands were going blue and she was shivering – in June.

We retreated to Eric to put the heater on, and Sarah hung her trousers out of the window. What was she wearing now? Wellington boots and knickers? These days panty lines to girlies are as important as Plimsoll Lines to mariners. I don't know if history reveals a Mr Panty. Worse still VPL stands for 'Visible Panty Line' which is very uncool and is certainly not 'wicked'. That was the good side of sinking into the mire – if you haven't got your trousers on – you can't have a panty line. Now, apparently, for the sake of fashion and removing the VPL, the thong is replacing the panty – a garment that seems to have been trimmed down and stolen from the world of Sumo wrestling. I have to admit that in my world, the thought of a Visible Underpanty Line causes me no anxiety whatsoever. On a cold winter's day I even have a magnificent Visible Long John Line (VLJL) which I flaunt with pride. Under no condition will I ever wear a thong – unless of course I take up Sumo wrestling.

Fortunately as we drove along the A3055 with Sarah's trouser legs flapping in the wind – her modesty and whatever she was wearing, was preserved by a Barbour jacket worn as a skirt.

'What shall I do?' All I had was half-baked directions and a half-naked adjudicator. I know, 'I won't phone "victim support", but I will phone the National Trust'. The National Trust has several important sites on the Island and *Eureka*, their top Island man, Tony Tutton, is a butterfly boffin and he immediately downed tools to come to our rescue.

By wearing her trousers over her wellies, Sarah returned to respectability – and by putting her hands over the heater, she restored her blood supply. It began to drizzle – I was pessimistic. Tony Tutton was bright and breezy – he was optimistic. He took us to a high cliff – 'Here we are,' he said with a smile, the short thick sward contained much ribwort, plantain and sea plantain – the food plants of the ***Glanville fritillary***. A huge area of cliff was breaking up and sinking – there were holes – depressions – mini cliffs and patches of turf. 'They live in colonies,' Tony told us, 'on a sunny day they would be flying all over the place here.' It was not a sunny day – the light drizzle kept drizzling and *they* were not flying anywhere. If I had been a ***Glanville fritillary*** I would have been under a very large leaf. 'There's a butterfly'; Sarah had found a butterfly – wings closed on a stem of grass – Tony sheltered it in his warm hands – the wings opened – it was a small, dark *fritillary* – the ***Glanville*** – a most attractive little butterfly – I would love to see it flying in sunlight. The butterfly was put back on its grass – Tony Tutton's optimism had been rewarded.

The ***Glanville fritillary*** was named after Eleanor Glanville – an enthusiastic amateur entomologist. When she died, her will was contested as some interested parties suggested that anybody obsessed with butterflies was mad. She sounds a very sane woman to me – if she had been worried by VPL I would have considered her mad – although in those days it would have been VBL – Visible Bloomer Line.

'You might as well see some of our other special butterflies while you are here,' Tony suggested, still smiling; it was still drizzling.

We travelled further along the coast road before stopping by a high area of downland. 'When the sun is shining this is a great place for the *small blue*. We might be lucky – I suspect on days like this they shelter in clumps of gorse.'

We climbed, puffed and grunted, at least I did, until we reached the gorse. We looked, stared, poked and rummaged – but there was nothing – just the odd, fast-flying moth. We gave up and returned to the track. Sarah stopped – her blue butterfly eyelashes fluttered. 'Here's a small butterfly.' She was right again – there on the long stem of seeding grass was a small butterfly, wings closed – but walking up the stem – a *small blue* going for a walk. Astonishingly there were several – all doing the same thing. Was this the equivalent of a Saga butterfly holiday? It was not bright enough to fly – nor dark or cold enough to hide – there was nothing else to do but walk up stems of grass.

'We'll try one more,' said Tony. This is the way to spot butterflies. Tony takes us: Sarah spots them: I tick the list – it's as simple as that. It was still drizzling as we moved inland to an area of grazed down. 'Up there,' said Sarah. Hooray – a butterfly that flies – a brilliant blue little butterfly, depending on horseshoe vetch – an *adonis blue* – the brightest blue of all our blue butterflies. It flew low and fast for twenty yards and disappeared.

Light drizzle turned into heavy drizzle; heavy drizzle turned into rain. We had been so lucky – three new butterflies in drizzle – and each one had been completely new to me. My original information had been right – we did see butterflies – there – here – and up there.

Hero Tony Tutton went back to his office. We found a 'Tea Room' to sip tea and watch the rain fall in stair-rods – southern England was awash. But it had been a successful butterfly day.

Sunday June 9th

What weather we have had. Low cloud and rain – wind and wet – when the rain comes in on the wind it seems so much wetter than when it simply drops on your head.

At last it has stopped. The farm tracks squelch – everywhere is dripping.

patient and she is happy – a happy, smiling, humming, laughing person is a rarity these days. Waiting for Booker she needed her patience. He'll be late for the funeral.

10.20am Where's Booker? Sarah assumed that she would be meeting a swash-buckling warrior – a journalist, writer, first editor of and contributor to *Private Eye*, inhabitant of 'The Old Rectory' etc. etc. That a tall, dark, bespectacled, intellectual would ooze into her life driving the latest and most expensive BMW. Instead – Booker arrived. He was driving a rust bucket worse than Sarah's in need of baler twine and sellotape. Booker got out – he too was in need of baler twine and sellotape, as well as windscreen wipers for his glasses. 'I'm sorry, I'm late,' he said, running his fingers through his tussled hair, 'I had to get ready for a funeral.' In that state was Booker going to be the body?

Ready for the funeral? Had he got a razor? If he had it was certainly blunt – he looked as if he had spent the night in the wardrobe and his unshaven chin had got the moth. 'But I have shaved,' he protested, as he lit a fag – oh, I had forgotten – this lover of freedom also loves the freedom to smoke, cough and wheeze.

To make up for lost time Booker roared away with his accelerator on the floor – if the rust bucket had a floor. Up into woods, the break-neck speed suddenly skidded to a halt in a dark, gloomy, shaded car-park. Booker parked his

motorised bucket next to one of equal vintage where the driver was reading a paper.

Forward and upward – through oak and ash and out onto the 'down'. Rich chalk grassland – with grasses and wildflowers – acres of almost wild garden. Have another fag Booker – he was a perambulating plume of pollution. What is he thinking of – he's already breathing heavily – wheezing and he's got to go up Mount Kilimanjaro with me – Africa's highest mountain – later in the year – unless the grim tobacco reaper intervenes first. Booker has wined and dined with some of the grandest in the land – or in his case whined and dined, and as we walked I had expected a recitation – a catalogue of EU evils with every stride, step or stagger – but this was a renewed Booker – he was effervescing with ecology – flowers, grasses and butterflies – 'Hod Hill is so important for butterflies – chalkland butterflies – the **common blue**, the **chalkhill blue**, the **adonis blue** – the **small copper** and of course the **marsh fritillary**' – pause, drag of fag, wheeze: 'there are orchids too – early purple, common spotted, pyramidal and bee': life cycle, history, childhood memories – pause, drag, wheeze; 'and the blue flowers, scabious, gentian, harebells, clustered bellflower, milkweed and of course Devil's bit scabious the food plant of the **marsh fritillary**', 'pause, drag, wheeze'. Sarah spotted a bee orchid: 'Can I pick it?' She was winding us up – I picked her a buttercup.

Once at the top, the wheezing stopped – 'Hod Hill is 471 feet high. Over there is Hambledon Hill 623 feet above sea level – over there is a spectacular hanging yew forest – the valley of the River Stour – a buzzard.' Where natural history stopped – history history started. 'Hod Hill was an Iron Age Fort – but in 43AD it became a Roman camp – Roman Britain spread from Dover to Dorset. Here we are on what was the western edge of the Roman Empire – look at all those hills, valleys and woods stretching eastwards – incredibly the Roman Empire spread eastwards as far as Iraq. The commander here was Vespasianus – remove his anus and he becomes the Emperor Vespasian.' 'Thank you Booker, have another fag.' 'No,' on he went, 'he followed star emperors – like Claudius and Nero – ideal candidates for the House of Commons today or EU Commissioners.' Well done Booker, I knew you wouldn't let me down. 'Titus Flavius Vespasianus was a remarkable man – he commanded the 2nd Legion – he subdued the Isle of Wight – before coming here.' 'Did he tread on any **Glanville fritillaries** there or see the **marsh fritillary** here?' Booker ignored me: 'As Emperor Vespasian he started the Colosseum and he got up early in the morning to work, as he enjoyed his siesta in the afternoon. It is said that his humour tended to take the form of coarse jokes.' 'Did he contribute to *Privaticus Optrexcicus* then?' I asked. Booker ignored me again.

'And then look at Hambledown Hill – marvellous – it was not just a hill fort – it was a cathedral.' Booker was bubbling – a new man: I had become exhausted and was starting to wheeze – Sarah's eyes had glazed over.

Unkindness to non-politicians is not one of my traits – Booker was fascinating – bringing a whole landscape alive and linking it to history – but where was the **marsh fritillary**? Nowhere to be seen. There were **cabbage whites**, **small tortoiseshells**, **meadow browns**, **common blues** – and what is that – smaller, lighter floppier – the **small heath** – what number is that? I have lost count. Oh, and then a light, bright, large butterfly – several of them – black, white and orange, a patchwork of coppers and duns $2\frac{1}{4}$ inches of beauty – the **painted lady** – all the way from North Africa – the Atlas Mountains – all of them migrants. But no **marsh fritillary** – Christopher thought the grasses were longer than in earlier days – did the **marsh fritillary** like land that had been grazed more heavily?

Back in the car park, Booker stroked his chin; 'I had better go and buy a razor.' 'Oh no – my bag!' Sarah cried out. Eric's passenger window had been smashed and Sarah's pink sparkly bag had been stolen containing her non-pink sparkly cheque book, plastic money, mobile phone and worst of all her bright blue eyelash liner – *phew* – I had left my wallet on the dashboard – *phew* – it was still on the dashboard – *phew* – I had left my mobile phone *on*, under the dashboard – *phew* – it was still *on* under the dashboard – *phew* – a stupid thief.

'Amazing!' announced Booker. 'I dreamt this would happen last night – only it was my car that was done – not yours – absolutely incredible.'

'What! You dreamt the car was broken into – you parked by a car containing a Dorset burglar and you didn't say anything. You warn us after it has happened?' – Christopher Booker – public school – Oxbridge – contemporaries in Parliament – in the Cabinet: now we know why the country is in such a mess.

My mobile was on – but Hod Hill and Hambledon were blocking all signals. We rushed to the village of Shillingstone – Sarah could just get through to the Dorset police if she stood near a brick wall and adopted a yoga position leaning left. 'Eric's been damaged and my bag's been stolen – my pink sparkly bag.'

Once Eric had been identified as a car the police seemed to lose all interest. 'Where was it parked?' 'At the car park at Hod Hill.' 'Oh cars are always being broken into up there.' Oh, thanks – why no warning notices then? Why no police patrols? Did they want a detailed description of the pink sparkly bag? No. Would they be coming out to see Eric? No. Were they too busy having political correctness courses to actually police? Were they too busy internet shopping to come to Shillingstone?

Once shaven, Booker was ready for his funeral, he had been good company. Eric was ready for the garage – Sarah was still trying to smile – but finding it difficult.

'What shall we do Sarah?' 'What?' The wind whistled through the broken window. I phoned Martin Warren at Butterfly Conservation. 'Martin, where can I find a *marsh fritillary*?' 'Oh, you've left it late Robin – they're nearly over in Dorset – they've been early this year. There's a colony right by the Cerne Giant – just below his right hand.'

Oh no, not the Cerne Giant – creeping around that giant hillside fertility symbol will make us look like a couple of perverts.

Some people in time gone by carved out giant white horses in the chalk hillsides of Dorset and Wiltshire – above Cerne Abbas they carved out a giant – a very immodest, naked giant – a giant that made bashful Victorian maidens even more bashful.

There he was – he looked pleased to us – I hope his good wishes were for Sarah and not for me. Most people view the Cerne Giant from a special car park on the outskirts of Cerne Abbas and from there we could see sheep fenced in with him – how could the *marsh fritillaries* survive?

The fence around the Cerne Giant is designed to keep the sheep in and people out – we had to get in – I pulled, heaved and pushed – trying to get my

leg over the numerous strands of barbed wire – without leaving behind what the giant was displaying so boastfully. One leg over – careful – don't slip – now the other leg – safety first. Sarah went up and over almost as if it wasn't there.

Below his right hand – nothing – just short grazed grass. Around his various other bits and pieces – nothing too; I jumped between two mounds – for the sake of decency – hillock to hillock – directly above me Sarah was standing on something that Victorian maidens would probably have avoided. There was nothing; we clambered out: half way over the wire the words of an old 1st World War song suddenly came to me, it was on an old 78" record of my parents – 'Where's the Sergeant Major? He's hanging on the wire. He's hanging on the old barbed wire he is – hanging on the old barbed wire.' I survived, just, leaving nothing on the barbed wire, and we walked through short but ungrazed grass with a yellow hawkweed growing in profusion – at last a non-blue butterfly, a non-small heath butterfly – a very tatty butterfly with fraying wings taking nectar from a hawkweed – surely the last **marsh fritillary** in Dorset – and certainly at that altitude and on chalk, a **marsh fritillary** that had never seen a marsh.

It had been a long hard day and a traumatic one for Sarah – but three new species – two unexpected and one desperately needed.

'I'll drive,' Sarah volunteered helpfully – it meant that I travelled nearly two hundred miles at 70 mph with the wind blowing continually on my face through the broken window.

Tuesday June 18th

Butterflies amaze me more and more with every passing day. Tenant Tim has cut a path through the flowering hay meadow of Telegraph Field – and there sunbathing with open wings on the short grass were four or five *painted ladies* – where were they yesterday?

Were they part of the windfall of wings at Hod Hill? Did they fly? Were they blown? How many *painted ladies* have suddenly dropped in on Britain all the way from North Africa and the Atlas Mountains? Incredibly *painted ladies* regularly migrate to all parts of Britain including Orkney and Shetland.

Small heaths were flopping too – fortunately for them they didn't have to fly from Hod Hill or even the Atlas Mountains – they will almost certainly have been born and bred on Telegraph Field – migrants fly – local yokel butterflies flop.

Wednesday June 19th

Eric amazes me more and more with every passing day – already the Freelander has travelled more miles than if it had migrated from the Atlas mountains and, oh dear – I can hardly catch my breath; we're off again. M11, A14, M6, M42, M5 – Oh dear – it is relentless, exhausting: 'Sarah where are we?' 'How should I know – you're driving.' Sarah has changed – somewhere in Dorset there must be a burglar with blue eyelashes. Thank goodness Eric's window has been repaired already.

Today it is the turn of the *small pearl-bordered fritillary* and again we are running out of time; the nearest sites to Cambridgeshire seem to be Gloucestershire or Dorset. The difference between the *pearl-bordered fritillary* and the *small pearl-bordered fritillary* is approximately $\frac{1}{8}$" in real measurement, or 3mm in comedy gobbledegook measurement. It should be simple then – once we have a ruler and both species in the fridge. The former has a wingspan of $1\frac{3}{4}$" – the latter $1\frac{5}{8}$" and of course the food plant of both are violets.

We were heading for the RSPB's Nagshead Nature Reserve in the Forest of Dean. The Forest of Dean suffered badly during foot and mouth – or more accurately, Ministry incompetence made the area suffer during foot and mouth by carrying out its normal, and often illegal policy of killing healthy animals, as a protective 'contiguous cull'. 'Sheep badgers' – the local shepherds had been allowed to let their sheep roam through the Forest for generations because of ancient rights – but suddenly their animals were rounded up and killed by the government; a government that loves foxes and animal badgers – but not farm livestock and human 'badgers'.

Apparently the human 'badgers' were now trying to replace their sheep – much to the chagrin of the suburbanised, homogenised incomers of the Forest of Dean, as well as those owners of holiday country cottages with urban minds; 'Say No to Roaming Sheep' proclaimed a poster – I will remember that next time my sheep get out. 'NO, NO, SIT, SIT.'

I had tired of Simon and Garfunkel for the 214th time and Jethro Tull for the 304th. Sarah had even tired of pulsating electronics and had tuned the Vibe throb knob to BBC Radio Gloucestershire – how exciting – a quiz: 'What have Adolph Hitler, Florence Nightingale and Horatio Nelson got in common?' The first telephone caller was very enthusiastic: 'I know – they're all dead.' Wrong answer – sadly we never did hear the right answer – were they drug addicts? Did they enjoy flower arranging? Were they butterfly lovers? We arrived at Nagshead and lost BBC Radio Gloucestershire.

The warden was out and so we wandered. At a small meadow there were **speckled woods**. Deep in the forest there were **speckled woods**. In the clearings along the rides – **speckled woods**. On a roadside verge, more **speckled woods**. Perhaps Hitler, Florence Nightingale and Nelson had all seen **speckled woods**?

What shall we do? We decided to head for Exmoor – which had several colonies of the sun-loving, brief flying **small pearl-bordered fritillary**. We fled to Exmoor. Exmoor was shrouded in low cloud and mist – it was like winter.

Thursday 20th June

A cooked breakfast at the Scott's. I wish I could have one every day – but I put fat on just thinking about it. I just managed to eat my bacon before being washed down by the slobbering tongues of two beautiful hound puppies; stag hounds – what incredible dogs. It was still cold and damp with the mist dripping from the leaves of the tall beech trees. Oh no – not again – the weather forecast warned of clouds coming in from the west – apparently mist over Exmoor is not counted as cloud – it is not even considered worthy of comment.

There was only one thing for it – leave Exmoor – to get rid of the mist and head for Somerset where I had been told of two *small pearl-bordered fritillary* sites.

What a relief – it was the right decision – winding down to Taunton from the moor we left the mist and hit sunlight and blue sky. I hoped the Mendips didn't have mist.

Back to motorway, the M5, more greenhouse gases – we now headed north.

The Mendips were not shrouded in mist, they were visible; they are formed by an attractive ridge of limestone running east/west high above the Somerset levels.

The walk to Crook's Peak – a rocky, craggy chunk of bare limestone saw *common blues* and yes – *speckled woods* flying and *meadow browns* and *small heaths* flopping. Where the hillside was open – the wind was cold – but where bush and scrub, gorse and thorn, gave shelter, the sun warmed and the butterflies flew – all that is except the *small pearl-bordered fritillary*. The sheep obviously like the short grazed turf – with plenty of wild thyme, eyebright, heather and stemless thistle. If I was a sheep I don't think I would want to eat a stemless thistle.

There was no wanted or expected butterfly – just a totally unexpected view – a wonderful view. From the top of Crook's Peak the Somerset Levels are mapped out below – hedges, ditches, willows, farms, meadows, grazing cattle and hay being made – with the M5 snaking along its western edge. Global warming and the Somerset Levels do not rest easily together – if the sea level rises it will be one of the earliest areas of England to flood – Crook's Peak could become rather crowded.

Blue sky and cool wind – a cool south-westerly wind – and there on the far south-western horizon – yet another belt of cloud edging nearer. At the top of Crook's Peak it was just visible; after walking to the bottom of Crook's Peak it was clearly visible. What shall we do? We must try one more site before we lose the weather – a hill fort.

Somerset seems to have a large number of hill forts. It either means that the early Somerset drinkers were very wild – or else they had to have somewhere safe to protect themselves from people who were even wilder. Who knows? I'm sure Booker knows – but sadly he is on the other side of the Mendips – no doubt lounging in his Old Rectory taking afternoon tea, while we are still searching for the *small pearl-bordered fritillary*. I wonder when the early men of Somerset started drinking cider?

The hill fort was at Dolebury Warren. Sarah's face dropped – the car park was a gloomy, shaded place – with mud, puddles and broken glass – car windows had been broken here already. Was burglar habitat the same in Somerset as Dorset?

We left Eric to his fate and climbed to the top of the fort – a high grassy bank with a large depression at its base. Who did the digging and who did the fighting and directing in those dim and distant days? I suppose the answer is the same as it has always been – those who dug then – are the same who would dig today – those who directed then – would be the same as who would direct today – no wonder all the hill forts were eventually over-run.

Butterflies – large butterflies – flying over flowering clovers and vetches – black and white butterflies – one of my favourites – the *marbled white*. I knew we would bump into it sooner or later – but I hadn't expected to see it today.

It was one more butterfly – but not a vital butterfly at this stage – the vital one was still the *small pearl-bordered fritillary*. There were now great chunks of cloud giving sun and shadow – the forerunners of sky-filled gloom.

Beyond the longer wall of the hill fort was a meadow of uncut, ungrazed grass, with small clumps of bramble. It looked promising – we wandered through it – *whites*, *browns* and *yellow brimstones* – *tortoiseshells* and *peacocks*, yes, and *painted ladies* – all attractive butterflies in their own right – but in the wrong place at the wrong time.

We began our return – my mind had already processed 'another blank day' which was rather unfair on the *marbled white*. Sarah started running and point-ing 'There it is – a *small pearl-bordered fritillary*.' Incredibly I was not looking at the butterfly – but at Sarah. Here was the urban girlie who at the start of the Butterfly Safari could hardly tell the difference between a cowslip and a cowpat, a toad from a toadstool and now she had identified a *small pearl-bordered fritillary* – and she was right.

It had been worth the wait. What a beautiful little butterfly – its wings were the colour of a deep, rich copper with black blotches and patches. It flew – glided – flew – found a friend – circled – flew – glided; we followed it through grass and round brambles like a couple of sorry drunks, smiling as if we had found gin – not butterflies. Forget the $\frac{1}{8}$" in real measurement – to me the *small pearl-bordered fritillary* has richer, redder wings that the *pearl-bordered fritillary*.

Then in brambles – another smaller moth-like orange-brown butterfly – to me it looked like an *Essex skipper* – the difference between an *Essex skipper* and a *small skipper* is very small indeed. So small that some people not trying to complete a Safari, simply split the difference and say they have seen a '*small/Essex*' it makes life much easier. The difference is simple – if you have a monocular as good as mine and a butterfly that is content to sit and sunbathe: the antennae of the **small skipper** are black above and orange below and the underside of the bobbles – sorry – *clubs* – are orange, the antennae and bobbles of the **Essex skipper** are all black.

Just like its human equivalent – Essex man (*Billericum orium necklaceum*) – the **Essex skipper** is expanding its range and the **Essex skipper** at Dolebury Warren would be on the very edge of its push south-westwards. Essex man's expansion is south-eastwards following its food plant – chips – across Spain.

Three more species seen. As Eric motorway hopped home – Sarah slept so soundly she was on the edge of a snore. I was wide awake – running on adrenaline – adrenaline from watching butterflies – previously I would not have believed it possible.

Friday June 21st

The longest day – I wish it was an even longer day – I need a sleep. Home late – up early – the sun is up and so will be the **black hairstreak**. Once more there is no time to lose as some colonies have already stopped flying.

Fortunately the journey was quite a short one – to an old wood – just north of Oundle. Oundle is an attractive town of stone – sandstone gives a much warmer appearance than some local stones. The town is dominated by its famous public school. Suddenly, as I was admiring the architecture Sarah screamed, my heart missed a beat – I braked – had I run over a cat – or even hit an old woman? I should have been watching the road. Neither – it was a scream of delight – not horror – Sarah had seen a shop selling dolls' houses. Dolls' houses? A shop selling nothing but dolls' houses – almost unbelievable. I said I would look round it – if Sarah would look round a shop containing nothing but cricket videos; we continued on our way.

The wood, owned by the local wildlife Trust was an area of old cow pasture gone wild – with grassy patches and clumps of bramble, hawthorn and blackthorn. A path had been mown into a sunny glade, alongside a large flowering path of bramble and there – on cue – a **black hairstreak** sucking nectar from a flower. The **black hairstreak** was of course brown and even the description '*hairstreak*' leaves much to the imagination. I have a friend with real hairstreaks – Emily Mayer is a Norfolk taxidermist, artist, sculptor – she has real hairstreaks – multi-coloured streaks of hair – the colours of the rainbow. **Hairstreak butterflies** simply have a few crooked white lines on the underside of their wings. As their wings are closed when they feed the streak is easily seen – but hairstreak? Not a very clever or descriptive name.

The *hairstreaks* are part of the Lycaenidae family which includes the '*blues*' and '*coppers*'. The *black* gets its name from tiny black dots on the underside of the wings – beautiful closed wings – brown, orange, black dots, white 'hairs' and a small black 'tail' on each hind wing – so delicate, so attractive and so easy to miss. The food plant is blackthorn; astonishingly, the eggs are laid on twigs – where they remain for the next nine months.

More *black hairstreak* appeared to feed – with several favouring flowering privet. They were very relaxed – is it possible to have 'tame' butterflies? The cut path was for a Trust open weekend – a public viewing of tame *black hairstreaks* – excellent.

What a restful change – instead of rushing and stressing, searching and climbing – here were tame butterflies on their nectar plants – entering on cue. Why couldn't the *small pearl-bordered fritillary* have taken note?

Another butterfly, a moth-like butterfly landed on a bramble flower – much larger than the *small/Essex*, it was a *large skipper* – number thirty-five – I think.

Monday June 24th

I have had two whole days to run the farm, run the CRT, earn a living, answer letters and watch my lawn grow – and it's off again – to Essex – Oh no! I wanted to see the *heath fritillary* in a beautiful little valley wood in Cornwall, on Duchy land. It is a rare, threatened butterfly which once thrived in coppiced woods – it needs glades, clearings and sunlight, as well as violets. I first saw it in Cornwall, several years ago and planned to return as part of the Great British Butterfly Safari. Sadly the Great British Weather Washout has put paid to this. Instead it has become the usual rush to see wings before they stop flying. So we are going to Essex.

'Cor blimey mate, Essex – will we see plenty of crims?' Replace 'Boyo' with 'mate' and Sarah was using the same accent that she uses in Wales.

'Cor blimey mate. Look at them – expensive houses for crims?' Kensington Pastures, Chelmsford – I'm sure there is not one criminal on the site – accountants, solicitors, bankers and bookies, yes, but not crims. It was a version of Virginia's McMansions – an assortment of large, new houses of different designs: Victorian, Georgian and Edwardian, dropped into a field and called luxury development. I am sure the words 'innovation', 'planning', 'best practice', and 'investment opportunity' must have been hovering somewhere in the vicinity. We were looking for 'Thrift Wood' – perhaps this site should have been called 'Extravagant Acres'.

But where was Thrift Wood? A post office would tell us where to find Thrift Wood. At Bicknacre not only does the post office have a counter where stamps can be bought and sold, but it also has a desk, with an estate agent in a suit, where new houses are bought and sold. 'Thrift Wood – yes – easy – left, left, left and right and you are at Thrift Wood.' It was very heartening – an estate agent interested in Thrift Wood – he must be a member of the Essex Wildlife Trust.

Left, left, left and right, and we were in the middle of a new housing estate and yes, the road was called Thrift Wood, next to Canons Close and The Grove. Never trust a man in a suit.

We found the real Thrift Wood after asking directions from a man wearing gardening clothes and with a dog on a piece of string. It was a wet wood, a wellies wood, and at the first clearing overflowing with brambles, several **heath fritillaries** were flying and gliding; they were about the same size as the **small pearl–bordered**, but darker and the wings were fringed attractively with white. There is another difference too – the food plant in Essex where the soil is acid is the yellow flowering common cow-wheat and not violets.

Suddenly Sarah screamed – Oh no, not again, there can't be a dolls' house shop in the middle of Thrift Wood surely? 'Help me – what shall I do?' She held her hand out in panic – her eyes were full of fear – this was the girl I had first met watching big game in Africa. 'What shall I do?' she begged again. Then I saw it – she was being savaged by an ant – a wood ant – at least $\frac{3}{8}$" long – twice as long as the garden ant. It had its jaws sunk well and truly into her skin, between two fingers. At great personal risk I pulled the beast off her and threw it away – I felt like David Livingstone. 'Don't panic, Sarah' I told her, 'you are lucky it bit you, it could have sprayed you with acid.' This was true – as wood ants can and do spray formic acid from their abdomen at their prey and at their enemies: she was lucky too as a large ant nest can contain up to 300,000 workers and the *Queens* can live for up to fifteen years. The jaws had marked her, but Sarah survived – survived in time to see the first **ringlet** of the summer – a dark velvet butterfly – a brown – with a string of rings – false eyes – on the underside of its wings and white centred dots on the top.

Two butterflies for the price of one.

In a nearby pub it really was 'cor blimey mate' – with gold chains, bracelets and a brand new Range Rover. 'I bet they're crims,' Sarah whispered too loudly. They were eating their food plant – fried and with plenty of tomato ketchup.

As we left they said – 'See you soon'. Really: where? What had we done?

As we returned the English McMansions looked no better from the opposite direction.

'It's criminal' said Sarah.

Wednesday June 26th

Hold tight – M11, A14, M6, M42, M5 – we're off again. Thank goodness for Sarah – without this blue eyelash flutterer, mud sinker, ant fighter, girl racer, throb FM listener, this Safari would have ground to a halt – exhaustion – miles, smiles, wings, weather forecasts, snacks and half-snatched snoozes – it would have been impossible for one person to keep the pace up – the distance, the hours would have all been too great.

Today there is rush again. If you believe the weather forecast there is cloud and drizzle coming in from the south-west and today I do believe the weather forecast. We are going to see the *large blue* – I hope – with Booker. He wants a second helping of butterflies.

I snoozed, Sarah cruised, at what speed I dare not look. We made good time under blue sky and a hot sun. The *large blue* butterfly has fascinated me for years; and if the *small copper* is the skylark this must be the 'osprey' of the butterfly world. It is, as its name suggests, large and blue, well *large* for a '*blue*' with a wing span of $1\frac{1}{2}$"; actually it sounds more impressive in madness measurement – 36mm. But in 1979 it was thought to have become extinct; its return was not natural like the osprey – but it has been successfully re-introduced.

The butterfly has a strange life cycle. The female lays its eggs on the flower bud of wild thyme and once they hatch, the caterpillars are carried off by ants – no, not biting wood ants – a special ant – *Myrmica sabuleti*. Perhaps the ants believe the caterpillars are their own grubs – who knows – who can think like an ant? Once inside the ants' nest the caterpillars busily scoff the ant grubs – while the ants in turn 'milk' the caterpillar of a sweet bodily secretion – tasting no doubt very strongly of liquidised grub: it is almost a type of third party cannibalism – or cannibalism made more acceptable and digestible. The butterflies emerge from the ant nests in June and July.

Extinction resulted from loss of habitat through ploughing and through the disappearance of grazing rabbits. The cycle of the *large blue* depends on both wild thyme and *Myrmica* ants and both the thyme and the ants need light and sun which result from grazing rabbits. When myxomatosis swept through Britain, rabbit grazing stopped, grass grew, ants and thyme were smothered and the *large blue* disappeared. Now where the *large blue* is back – if there are no rabbits, the conservationists graze the sites with cattle or sheep – producing not only *large blue* butterflies but beautiful beef and lamb from herb-rich grazing.

The meeting place for Booker was the National Trust's Collard Hill, not far from Glastonbury. Meeting time for Booker was 12.00.

12.00 No Booker. Where's Booker?

12.15 Where's Booker? Phone Booker – no reply.

12.30 The rust bucket lurches into view – it is almost as noisy as a Formula One Ferrari. Sarah's taste in clothes is sophisticated. My taste in clothes is practical. Booker's taste in clothes is non-existent; he looked as dog-eared as his butterfly Bible – *Butterfly Book for the Pocket* by Edward Sanders (published 1937). Who knows, perhaps the book and the jacket arrived together as a job lot.

The National Trust has a policy of open access for Collard Hill – whether that will suit the *large blue* remains to be seen. Collard Hill is really a high ridge of limestone, an escarpment, and the view from the top made the rush, the wear and tear and even 'Vibe FM' seem worthwhile – valleys, fields, woods, water and haymaking. There is still nothing that can match the magnificence of England in full summer. At every turn from the summit we could see hills – the Blackdowns, the Poldens, the Quantocks, the Mendips, the Brendons and Glastonbury. Again the view emphasised the inadequacy of the word green – there are so many of them – lush, loud, subtle, gentle, fading, brilliant, dark, light – but all green.

Booker added geography and the points of the compass to history, and for once his lungs were breathing clean air – air carrying the scent of mown hay, growth, warmth and a hint of the sea.

The sun was hot – the blue sky was broken by wisps and patches of white cloud – this was pure summer – without the threat of drizzle from the southwest. The weather forecasts have got it wrong.

I could have stayed sitting in the sun taking in the view, re-connecting with nature – servicing my senses all afternoon – but we had a butterfly to see – a completely new butterfly for Booker. I went ahead of the other two anxious and eager – the grass seemed very short. I went on to the next property, where the habitat looked perfect. The trouble with going down is you have to climb up again.

There was nothing – various others – floppers and even hoppers as there were grasshoppers in the longer grass – I went back to National Trust land. I didn't like the way Sarah and Booker were smiling – they were definitely looking smug. 'Have you seen one?' I asked. 'Of course we have – that's what we came here for. I did call you Robin but you didn't come.'

'Yes, she did Page – I can confirm that. The butterfly was down there – and flew off towards some bracken at 2 o'clock – that's the direction – not time.' Booker was sounding like an EU directive. Sadly I believed them, as they were both grinning like cats that had claimed the cream.

We moved further down the escarpment where there were clumps of bramble and gorse as well as 'herb-rich grass'. Other butterfly twitchers had arrived – a photographer in a Budweiser T-shirt carrying his camera and huge lens already on its tripod – at every shadow or rustle he twitched and searched – sometimes breaking into a trot. 'The original Nature Nerd' thought Booker. 'There it is' – Sarah had seen another – flying low and fast in the breeze – Nature Nerd broke into a gallop and disappeared into the distance in hot pursuit. Three ladies were enjoying their day – they had come from the Isle of Wight. Sarah was in top form – she had found another – what a beautiful deep blue – there was a clatter and a bang – Nature Nerd had arrived. 'Excuse me – excuse me', he wanted to take a photograph – we excused ourselves and left.

We were not deserting the *large blue* after such a short stay – we were moving on to another nearby site – Green Down – owned and managed by the Somerset Wildlife Trust – access is by permit only.

It was a beautiful flowering meadow of springy half-grazed turf – it was south facing and warm with abundant banks of flowering thyme – and ants. *Large blues* flew and settled. What a place – petals and wings – colours and scents – a meadow that emphasises what we have lost – just as much as it symbolises what can be saved. Anne Moxley – a volunteer and Hugh Dixon a warden, were quite rightly proud of their meadow. At one time access to Green Down was almost unrestricted, but incredibly some visitors tried to steal the *large blue* – not just the butterflies but also the eggs, caterpillars and even the ants. 'When does a Nature Nerd become a butterfly burglar?' Bookend had the answer. 'Once they have ticked all the names on their list – their obsession is so great that they actually want to own the butterflies.' He could be right.

90

We followed Booker back to his residence – or more accurately we tried to follow Booker back to the Old Rectory at Litton – but he roared away like the old cartoon character Dick Dastardly in *The Whacky Races.* We eventually arrived at the Old Rectory. A Rector is of a higher social and spiritual standing than a vicar; a better class of cleric and so I suppose an Old Rectory is more desirable than an Old Vicarage. I hope the resident of the Old Rectory at Litton remains in residence – not like the resident of the Old Vicarage at Grantchester – my next village – he was required to take up residence elsewhere – behind barbed wire and very high walls. That could prove the point – an Old Rectory resident usually appears to be a better class of person than someone living in an Old Vicarage.

Tea and biscuits at the Booker residence was almost civilised – with Wimbledon on widescreen telly (complete with Sky) severely denting the Booker image. Well, tea with the delightful Mrs Booker was civilised – the uncivilised element kept getting up, tea in hand, 'I've got cricket nets – where's my bat? … where's my box? … where's my cap?' – before roaring off into the Somerset summer evening. 'He's forgotten his boots,' said Mrs Booker – the image was restored.

We arrived back at the farm at dusk – a warm, gentle dusk as a beautiful day slowly died. I had just one more task – to visit the brook meadows to check the cows and their calves – another sixteen-hour day.

Rabbits were out grazing – in the half light – and then I saw something that I had never seen before – as the rabbits rambled back to the long vegetation near the brook – they were ambushed by four or five little fox cubs – barely the size of cats. The rabbits responded with turns and acceleration and easily got away – the cubs clearly thought it was great fun.

What makes the incident even odder is that this 'earth' with small cubs is just 50 yards away from another earth with half-grown cubs. I have never know two occupied earths to be so close together before, or two earths to have such a difference in the cub size of their litters.

Thursday June 27th

Too early – Rachael is upset and crying on the phone. A fox or foxes have broken into the goose shed and killed the old gander and his befriending daughter. The bodies were only partially eaten – the fox could get in through a small hole but could not get the bodies out.

Friday June 28th

Warm again. At nine I walked with Sarah to the old railway line. We have done this several times hoping to see **marbled whites**, as a CRT member has tried to introduce this attractive butterfly. Slowly the flowers of high summer are opening – but there are no **marbled whites** to be seen. Suddenly – white wings. It was a false alarm: the butterfly was a solitary **green-veined white**. To show the madness of the year, my various books claim that late June and early July is the only period of the summer that the **green-veined white** does not fly. This particular **green-veined white** is saying, 'yes we do'. Compared with some butterflies the food plant of the **green-veined white** can almost be classified as 'health food' – so check your watercress for munching caterpillars next time you include it in a salad. My old father always insisted that if a caterpillar or maggot was accidentally eaten it was no major problem. Whether in cabbage, cauliflower, watercress or Stilton cheese – the caterpillar or maggot was basically a moving version of what it had been eating and so, why be cautious in bad creepy crawly years? I can still see him on one occasion eating Stilton that was almost alive. He stuck to his guns and ate the green-veined cheese maggot mansion with a smile – I had to leave the room.

A young green woodpecker – obviously not yet an expert flyer – almost crash-landed on to Sarah's head – fortunately she did not see it or hear it. If it had hit, then it would have been a case of demanding the kiss of life – possibly for the woodpecker. If an ant on the finger is an emergency – then a woodpecker chick on the head would be a disaster.

One minor disaster to British wildlife would be a world shortage of peanuts. Today a young sparrow was actually perching on the peanut holder, its wings quivering, begging for pecks of peanuts from its mother. I hope this dependence on junk bird food does not cause obesity in birds; the only winners would be Britain's bird-scoffing domestic cats which already, it is estimated, scoff 270 million wild birds and animals a year – many of them protected species.

Today marks another step deeper into bumpkin land for Sarah – she has been given a cucumber plant. She has put it in the garden – after hacking a space in the weeds, and named it Colin.

Saturday June 29th

Another bright start to the day – blue sky and warm sun, although there is still a cool edge to the wind.

Mick arrived early as we have to move the sheep back to the brook meadows. When we brought them up to be sheared we could hardly get them into the trailer – with pushing and shoving, we managed to squeeze them in. Taking them back – minus their fleeces – there was plenty of room. The shearer, Alec, is a young farmer who originates from two or three villages away. He is tough, articulate and obliging with not an ounce of fat on his body – unlike my old ewes; he has sheared over 7,000 sheep so far this summer. Even with electric clippers it takes a great deal of strength and stamina. I declined his kind invitation to shear one – with my hair in its present condition it would have looked like two woolly sumo wrestlers having a disagreement. Because of the lack of livestock, following foot and mouth, he is having to travel as far as Yorkshire to do his shearing this year.

It is amazing to see a young Englishman doing such hard, physical work these days. A friend, three miles away as the crow flies, cannot get students to cut his asparagus, pull his raspberries, or pick his alpine strawberries – consequently large proportions of his crops are going to waste. The simple fact is that British students will no longer do physical work; in previous years he has employed young people from Eastern Europe who have worked hard and been reliable. This year the Home Office will not let them in – the plight of the small farmer is of no interest to the bureaucrats.

Once the sheep were settled we went to the railway line again – surely there would be a *marbled white* today?

There are plenty of nectar-giving flowers for butterflies now – knapweed, field scabious, various vetches and ragwort. There were *meadow browns* and *ringlets* flopping about – *large skippers* with a totally different understanding of flight and then, suddenly, at last, a *marbled white* – flying, gliding and settling with its wings open. What a beautiful butterfly, containing so much beauty for just two colours. If the *large blue* is the osprey of the butterfly world, the *marbled white* must be the zebra, and of course its caterpillars eat grass – favouring cock's foot, red fescue and sheeps fescue.

Entirely in keeping with entomology, the *marbled white* is classified as a 'brown', being in the same family (Satyridae) as the *meadow brown* and the *ringlet*. Its other oddity is that the female lays her eggs while flying over the food plants – a bouncing bomber of the butterfly world – a habit it shares with the ringlet.

It was marvellous seeing this one, solitary butterfly, I hope plenty more appear. It was one of Gordon Beningfield's favourite butterflies; the successful introduction of the *marbled white* to the CRT's Lark Rise Farm would have given him so much pleasure. I wonder when, or if, the **marbled white** was in this part of East Anglia. I phoned Betty Beningfield to tell her the good news. We will not be able to say that the introduction has been successful for three of four years, when, and if numbers increase.

Before clouds rolled in, five great tits were having a communal bath in the bird drinker, such a splashing gathering can only be called a 'titillation'.

One of them then managed an astonishing feat; it appeared to lie on the washing line with one wing stretched out in the sunlight and its tail fanned. After five minutes it switched round and stretched out the other wing.

Cricket was cancelled this afternoon, the opposition could not raise a team – the gradual demise of this beautiful game is another sign of the times. With cricket now absent in many schools, non-asparagus picking youngsters are also growing up without cricket. Cricket is a great social mixer; the average village team contains people from many different classes, races and backgrounds; perhaps that is why politicians and educationalists don't like it – cricket does more for social harmony than they do. At the moment our team contains a broken-down car retriever, a farm seed developer, a student teacher, a Christian researcher into the Holy Spirit, an air traffic controller and four Mr Patels; running a variety of post offices and garages. The only Patel Christian name, sorry, Hindu name that I can pronounce is Kevin.

Perhaps it is a good thing cricket was cancelled. In the last game I managed to achieve a first in my long and far from illustrious village career – batting at number two I was 'run out' without facing a ball. What is worse – I called for the run – speed of mind is obviously far faster than speed of body.

Instead of cricket I followed an enjoyable family tradition. At two in the afternoon I was sound asleep in the armchair when there was a sudden knock on the door. It was two strangers bearing gifts – well they were not strangers – but for the sake of continuing friendship I will not name them. They had a cool box with them, was it time for a picnic? Had they got ice-cold bottles of organic cider? Or were they giving me a bottle of chilled champagne to celebrate the arrival of the **marbled white**?

They opened the cool box; inside were, *thirty more* **marbled whites**! Bill and Ben are butterfly men, they love butterflies, they are not butterfly burglars or nature nerds – they are butterfly conservationists. They simply decided that a site they knew had a surplus of **marbled whites** – it was not managed for butterflies, at times Rail Track hardly seems to manage for trains – and so they decided to boost the **marbled whites** of Lark Rise Farm.

We released them close to where I had seen this morning's butterfly. With the sun on their wings, movement and flight quickly came and they lifted off into the breeze – only to flutter down thirty or forty yards away.

When people with white coats, beards, sandals and PhDs undertake experiments like this, it is called 'scientific research'. When unqualified enthusiasts like Bill and Ben do the same thing, but lacking the white coats, beards, sandals and PhDs it is called irresponsibility. I have had the privilege of meeting many irresponsible Bills and Bens – George Adamson with lions, John Aspinall with gorillas, Tony Fitzjohn with black rhino, Dot Eaton with Dormice. And B… with c…… And now Bill and Ben with butterflies. The amazing thing about this is that the 'irresponsible' ones have nearly always been more successful than the scientists.

Perhaps this should be the subject of a PhD. Why are so many unqualified wildlife enthusiasts better at managing wildlife than 'experts' or 'scientists'? I think that I already know the answer – too many 'nature nerds' go on to become scientists and set themselves up as 'experts'.

Sarah phoned from London in the evening; she had missed a thrilling day in Bumpkin land. I told her the good news that, with watering, I thought Colin the cucumber was pulling through a crisis. Strange that, surrounded by her London friends, it seemed as if she didn't want to talk about cucumbers.

Sunday June 30th

The sun came with the dawn again – but no time to check the **marbled whites**. Today is another Dorset day for the CRT, with Nigel and Tim Scott the tenant farmer of Lark Rise Farm. At least it means there are no handbags to be stolen – I hope.

We were going to Dorset to look at another farm which might be suitable for the Gordon Beningfield Memorial Appeal. During the course of the day we could stop at Martin Down, in Wiltshire, to see three butterflies; the **white admiral**, the **dark green fritillary** and the **silver washed fritillary**. Then, if time and weather permitted, a quarry on the island of Portland was good, so I was told, for **silver-studded blues**.

Early Sunday morning driving on the M25 and the M3 was almost a pleasure – but the only thing of significance to be seen at Martin Down was a piebald pony that insisted on following us around like a dog – a rather big dog.

There were plenty of flopping **ringlets** and **meadow browns**, and shining **marbled whites** – are they following me too? But no new species. The woodland was very attractive with managed rides and clearings, if the weather warms, then the target butterflies must be there.

As we returned to the car park, a model plane, with a roaring engine was looping the loop just beyond the cars. A model aircraft in a National Nature Reserve drowning the songs of several larks? I suppose this is the government's idea of 'multi-functional countryside use', in other words 'theme park Britain', where the townies can come and play. Perhaps someone with a shotgun ought to practice clay pigeon shooting in the National Nature Reserve – as his or her 'right', shooting model aircraft.

The farm near Dorchester – very near Dorchester – had many features that are perfect for the Gordon Beningfield Memorial Farm – and several features that are far from perfect. We must give it a lot of thought.

Clouds blew in; the wind still had a cool cutting edge and so **silver-studded blues** would have to wait for another day. Instead we walked around the Dorset Wildlife Trust's Kingcombe reserve with its ancient meadows in full bloom with orchids, knapweed, clover, various hawkweeds, flowering thistles and many more.

Appallingly it was a junk food day, with Nigel and Tim eating burgers, after their earlier fried breakfasts. I refuse to eat burgers after an incident in which dissident farmers blockading a port in the north-west discovered a container lorry full of German cow udders travelling to a major English burger factory. The first question is – why were German cow udders coming into England, via Ireland? Something a bit strange there.

The second question is – why are German cow udders put into some British burgers anyway? Answer – much British beef is grown so quickly that it is fatless. Consequently fat has to be added to bind the burger together – and what can that fat sometimes be? German cow udders. As a result conversation in burger bars should include; 'Can I have an udder burger please?' And when that one is finished; 'Can I have a n'udder udder burger please?' I think I will make do with a cucumber sandwich.

Oh dear – it was a completely blank butterfly day.

JULY

Wednesday July 3rd – The Royal Show

With farming still in the Doldrums I thought I had better go to the Royal Show – for the sake of farming solidarity. Different place – different area – I may even tick a new butterfly- the **gatekeeper** should be a common butterfly to emerge any day now. But sadly the Royal Show seems to be in the hands of agribusiness – the same people who are turning agri'culture' into an industrial process and who are spraying and cultivating the wildlife of farmland into oblivion. Many of the Royal Show's Establishment will be the same people who run the National Farmers Union, and who supported the government in its cynical slaughter of 10 million farm animals during last year's foot and mouth. I hope these same people volunteer for slaughter when they get anything contagious, my preferred choice is vaccination.

My choice of the Third Day of the show managed to avoid the spectacle of the farming leaders bowing and scraping to the politicians on Day One. I actually had an invitation to a reception hosted by the Secretary of State – Margaret

SENIOR CITIZENS
CHILDREN
HALF PRICE

Becket – the flashing gummed Caravan Queen – yes, as far as I'm aware her only claim to countryside knowledge before getting the top political farming job was ownership of a caravan – and where was her caravan during the peak of the foot and mouth crisis so it was said? In France. I turned down the invitation – the red mist would have descended – sadly some of the Pimms sipping, limp-wristed individuals who claim to lead farming seem unable to see red. Through an all enveloping mist of political sycophancy, what they appear to see is the shining lure of a knighthood out on the other side. We did not arrive until well into the afternoon and there are no reductions for latecomers. Sixteen pounds for two hours seemed rather excessive and so I managed to be admitted as a senior citizen and Sarah as a child.

Sarah had never heard of the Royal Show. Why should she – she has never wanted to buy a tractor for use in Hammersmith, Sloane Square or Kensington High Street. Nevertheless I bet her that she would buy something, and convinced that she had no need for a combine harvester or a muck fork – she accepted. The first and largest pavilions to meet the eye once in the Royal Show ground are those belonging to the supermarkets – with each one vying to be grander than its rival.

It is astonishing – why are the supermarkets allowed into the Royal Show in the first place? It is the buying power of the supermarkets that is distorting the God of the 'Free Market' thus helping to destroy the family farm in Britain, the mainstay of farming for generations. Those who work in supermarkets don't seem to care – as long as they get their monthly salary cheques. Those who shop in supermarkets don't seem to care as long as their food is cheap. The only people who care are the families of those who not only pull the plug on supermarkets, but life itself. With a farming suicide every six days there are those who pay a very high price for cheap food. The families left behind continue to pay a price for months, even years; they pay in grief and tears.

We visited smaller friendlier stands; one urging all comers to march on September 22nd in London; another offering comfort and support to all farming families in distress and another selling vibrating cushions – what – vibrating cushions! With each purchase of a vibrating cushion came the promise of a vibrating hairbrush. What is going on? Is this the age of the gay tractor driver – vibrating cushion, handbag and plug-in hair curlers?

Sarah's bankcard hand trembled at the eyelash curling counter. Eyelash curlers have always been important on British Farms – why else would they be at the Royal Show? Not only did her hand tremble at the food tent – but also bags

opened and filled with cheese, sausages, raspberry juice, oatmeal biscuits and assorted exotic dips. She still claimed to win her bet of course – who had to pay? I did. And what is my enduring memory from this celebration of British Farming? A vibrating cushion.

Thursday July 4th

Doesn't time fly when you are stress eating? The weather has been appalling. The temperature has plummeted to almost October levels and rain came as soon as the hay was cut. It now lies damp and mouldering – I sit frustrated and smouldering, waiting for the sun. Another popular British myth is that it is easy to lose weight in the summer if you eat seasonally – ho, ho, ho. Asparagus must be accompanied by lamb chops, an array of vegetables, plus lashings of mint sauce and white sauce – white sauce – healthy eating? I think not. Then come salads, plus high protein caterpillars of the *large* or *small white* – together with mixed vegetables in mayonnaise, potato salad in mayonnaise, salad cream, meat pie – together, of course with new brown bread and soft, fresh English butter.

Then come strawberries and raspberries – very 'healthy food' the way I eat them, covered with sugar, condensed milk and ice cream. If there is no ice cream then straight dairy cream and evaporated milk make an excellent substitute. If I was a caterpillar I think I would get to the chrysalis stage very quickly. So stress eating, waiting for the sun is not such a bad thing after all. Today the weather forecasters claim there will be a brief break, with real sun and high cloud, so it is off to Minsmere.

Minsmere is a bird reserve in Suffolk belonging to the RSPB. It is particularly famous for avocets – a graceful black and white wading bird, but not only does Minsmere have feathered wings, but it also has butterfly wings in the shape of the *silver-studded blue*; it has other butterflies too – but the *silver-studded blue* is the one I want to see today. The problem is that the appalling weather is gradually leading to a wing jam of butterflies – a long list of butterflies to see – but no sunshine to bring them out and see them. Those butterflies that should be flying about now and joining the Great British Butterfly Safari tick list are the *dark green fritillary*, the *silver washed fritillary*, the *high brown fritillary*, the *purple emperor*, the *white admiral*, the *northern brown argus*, the *large heath*, the *small mountain ringlet* and the *Lulworth skipper* – which means I need to be in three places at once, several hundred miles apart, next time the sun shines. At this rate Eric, the girlie freelander, will start falling to pieces when and if we get a hot spell.

To make the challenge of the *silver-studded blue* even more interesting the local BBC regional programme – *Look East* – wants to come too. Their reaction to news of the Great British Butterfly Safari was totally opposite that of their Lords and Masters at national BBC2 'Oh that will be of great interest to our viewers, what butterfly will you be doing next?' 'Can we come too?'

I felt confident as we wound our way through Suffolk. A straight road in the

Suffolk countryside is as rare as a straightforward politician in the House of Commons. Sarah had her eyelashes painted blue today; the **silver-studded blue** must be attracted to them.

The *Look East* camera crew were in the car park when we arrived. In days gone by four, five or even six people turned up with each camera; at Minsmere there were just two – Mike Liggins the presenter-cum microphone holder – and Andy Parsons, a rather cheerful camera man. Oh no – don't tell his bosses – Andy is also politically incorrect and took no time at all to tell me that he, and bus loads of friends would be going on the Countryside March on September 22nd. We were joined, in turn by a young RSPB warden – Aaron Howe.

On turning off the main track – disaster – the first butterfly I saw, flopping along was a **grayling** – a butterfly I dont want *Look East* to film today. It became a case of 'don't mention the **grayling**'. There were plenty of other floppers – **meadow browns** and **ringlets** – and so the **grayling** simply wasn't seen.

Through pines and bracken we came to an open area of heather 'lowland heath' with the bell heather already on flower. Three red deer hinds were browsing – but when we stopped – they made off quietly into the woodland. Already the early sunlight was turning to haze and cloud and the warm wind was cooling – would we be in time?

There was no need to worry – the **silver-studded blue** spends much of its time on dull days sitting on top of clumps of bell heather with its wings open.

Some butterflies might travel hundreds – even thousands of miles on migration – the average **silver-studded blue** hardly travels twenty feet in the course of a day – why can't all 56 species of butterfly behave like this?

It was a very attractive little butterfly and very obliging. The camera was able to get some stunning shots – with Andy getting down to butterfly level and in turn Aaron and I were able to say the right, trite things – as required. Our ten minutes would be cut down to two and a half – never mind, on television the image is the message – the words are like background wallpaper – they are there, reeled off, peeled off and quickly forgotten. Poor Sarah was not needed, much to her delight – instead, as the temperature fell her hands turned as blue as her eye-lashes and felt like ice – is this safari turning her into a blue butterfly?

Like its big relative the **large blue** the **silver-studded blue** has a strange relation-ship with ants. The eggs are laid singly on the woody stems of the food plant from July to August – and remain eggs until the following spring. They are then protected by black ants who feed on a sugary liquid produced by the larvae through special glands – the ants may even pick up the larvae and take them to ant chambers beneath rocks or stones. One species gets protection – the other gets food. In the world of *Homo sapiens* it is rather like the relationship between politicians and donors – one receives money and in return the other gets favours. With ants and butterflies it is called a symbiotic relationship; with politicians I call it corruption (a *sin*biotic relationship), although the politicians themselves call it 'part of the democratic process'; they would, wouldn't they!

Politicians and political parties receive donations from big business, multi-national companies, vested interests and supermarkets. It is these groups who like developing 'lowland heath' – 'useless land' – with houses, industrialised food pro-duction, shopping centres and forestry – consequently the **silver-studded blue** has lost more than 60% of its habitat over the last 50 years. If only the butterfly could divert its natural sweetener from ants to politicians.

Sunday July 7th

Another long day ahead, but, fortified, ready for the journey by scoffing for breakfast some of the traditional pork sausages bought at the Royal Show. Fried, not grilled, they were delicious. There are plenty of 'health food' books on sale these days; perhaps I should write one on 'unhealthy eating' and start off with fried pork sausages. Perhaps too, in order to recover from all the frenetic chasing about on the butterfly safari, next year I ought to go on The Great British Food

Safari – sampling the traditional food of Britain. Oh dear – what chapter titles it could have – 'Troughing through the Trossacks' – 'The Trencherman's Guide to Cheese' and 'Fat is Fun'. Despite the worst excesses of the supermarkets, health and safety officials, junk food chains and the homogenisation of both food and people, we still have a surprising amount of top quality traditional and seasonal food.

Sadly, when dealing with butterflies, there are more problems than simply thinking about breakfast. The problem today is that it is not a butterfly day. Suddenly a traditional Herefordshire farm is on the market – it has houses, fine old buildings and two hundred and fifty acres of ancient grassland – some of it on the flood plain of the River Dore. Now what does the 'efficient farmer' do with such a farm – he or she obeys the will of the great Caravan Queen of course – 'be efficient', 'be competitive – on the world market', 'be a government-inspired hooligan – tart up the farmyard and sell it off as executive houses or holiday homes and plough up the old pastures on the flood plain and grow potatoes'. All that stored up fertility next to the river – years of fertility – generations of fertility – centuries of stored up fertility – it could enable a few bumper crops of spuds to be grown. With good yields the flood plain potatoes may even be as cheap on the supermarket shelves as those imported from Egypt – grown by peasants on worn out soil with water squeezed from the Nile. So – to be efficient and competitive in the 'global market place' screw part of Herefordshire, to match the ruination of the Nile Valley and I suppose this is what the Caravan Queen might call 'working towards a sustainable future'.

So flowers, butterflies, landscape and tradition were being sold in Herefordshire and the CRT thought it ought to be involved – what price butterflies? What price potatoes? I decided to travel down to Herefordshire to have a look – so the sun came out strongly – the first time for days and with each weary mile I thought 'how many *fritillaries*, *white admirals*, *purple emperors* are flying today?'

Shropshire, Herefordshire, Gloucestershire and the Welsh borders are hidden Britain at its best. It is another world – Ross-on-Wye, Ludlow, Tewkesbury, Much Marcle, Dowton on the Rock, Little Dewchurch et al. Why should old countryside, old England be ruled by the people of new Milton Keynes, new Cumbernauld, new Harlow and New Labour? Why should urban millions boss rural thousands – that is not democracy – it is domination.

The farm at Turnastone was wonderful – grasses, butterflies and horseflies – not even horses want horseflies. The old three-storey farmhouse had house martins nesting under the eaves and the farm buildings were ideal – for farming –

for cows, sheep and hay or for executive houses and holiday cottages. Working farm or stockbroker's hideaway? That is the question. Food production and wildlife tolerance, or potatoes and lifestyle living?

The CRT had been told of the impending sale by Ian Hart – a lover of trees, flowers and butterflies. He eats of course – but not potatoes grown in Egypt or on Herefordshire flood plains. 'I'm here because I want to save it,' he said. 'On a normal sunny day like this I would be looking for butterflies.' Did he have to say that? 'What butterflies?' I muttered. Sarah's blue eyelashes fluttered. Automatic responses to the word 'butterflies' – what strange people we are becoming. It got worse; 'The woods round here have **silver-washed fritillaries**, **dark green fritillaries** and **white admirals**'. A photographer from *The Daily Telegraph* had joined us to warn the world of possible impending doom.

As he clicked here and clicked there – with Ian looking serious, philosophical, angry and indignant – the clock ticked and the sun moved across the sky and all around us in the woods the butterflies would be flying.

We walked across fields and meadows. We inspected an antique drainage system designed to increase the fertility of the old meadows. Today meadows are 'improved' by drainage – taking water away from grass. In earlier times the meadows were improved by taking water to the grass – to add moisture and silt. I know which version of 'improvement' I prefer.

With each stride the shadows lengthened. Then there were the cottages – one empty and one with a tenant. The 84-year-old tenant had been running the post office and village shop from his house for years. It had a garage too – with two ancient pumps standing in the garden and delivering the petrol in gallons.

The guide price for the farm is a million – verging on £1.1 million. The CRT hasn't half a million so how can we buy it? As I wandered around the farm I thought of butterflies. As I wandered round Ian's little wood looking for butterflies I thought of the farm – could we or should we try to buy it?

Ian too had been waiting to escape to see butterflies. He loves them so much that he actually bought a wood for them. A wood for woodland butterflies. He has planted trees and cut trees down. He has created clearings to let the light in and allowed dense canopy to grow to keep the light out. As a consequence there were shafts and pools and puddles of light – shifting with the leaves, and there were arches and avenues and arcades of shade. In the gloom the woodland flowers had faded when spring changed to summer and the leaves turned light to shade. Violets had been the early flowers; the flowers of high summer were bramble, enchanters nightshade, and strings of sweet-scented honeysuckle. What

butterfly can resist feeding on the nectar of bramble; what **white admiral** can fail to lay its eggs on honeysuckle? No less than six ***fritillaries*** have violets as their food plant.

As we looked high for ***white admirals***, rich golden wings flew low over the bramble flowers and settled. The ***silver-washed fritillary*** is a large butterfly – the largest ***fritillary*** with a wingspan of 2¾". A butterfly of silver and gold – fluttering over nectar and blossom – a perfect combination.

The blue eyelashes had partially worked – one butterfly out of three possibles, when I had expected none. It's time I counted the list again; 41 seen, 15 to go – at least.

It's time I counted the CRT's money again – £600,000 short of £1.1 million. It was a wonderful farm – I think I will make a bid with the money I haven't got; something will turn up.

Monday July 8th

7.15am Eric the postman came. All the bids for Turnastone Farm must be made by Wednesday. We will make a bid – well over a million and hope.

The rest of the day was dominated by wings – closed and open. The phone rang at 7.30am – Colin Shawyer was at the CRT's Warners Corner field. For years he has almost been The Hawk and Owl Trust – promoting and helping birds of prey – particularly the barn owl. The barn owl is not a butterfly and the *only* thing the two have in common are eyes. The barn owl has beautiful eyes and the **peacock** butterfly has beautiful eye markings on its open wings. The **purple emperor** has a large 'owl' eye too – on the underside of its closed wings. The 'predator' butterfly eye is supposed to deter predators – perhaps it does – that is why there are still so many butterflies.

On second thoughts the barn owl and the butterfly have *two* things in common – they both fly over the long grasses of the Warners Corner field looking for food; the barn owl for mice, voles and shrews, the butterfly for the nectar of thistles, daisies and clover. Butterflies have been flying the field for as long as anybody can remember – **large whites**, **small whites**, **peacocks**, **small tortoiseshells**, **meadow browns, ringlets, small heaths** and **brimstones**. Barn owls stopped flying the field and now only those with longer memories can remember them. They stopped in the 1960s – suddenly those white, hovering, flickering, silent, ghostly wings disappeared. The only things left were memories and ghosts. Memories of better times and moonlit shadows, that could have been the white owls back – or ghosts. The white owls died; sprayed away by the poisoned mist that washed over the land – to protect it – to poison it. DDT built up in fragile bodies and a long hard winter of ice and iron-hard fields did the rest.

I never expected to see the white owls back without a re-introduction of hand-reared birds. Colin Shawyer arrived after the birth of the CRT with nest boxes, and new meadowland created great swathes of grass for butterflies and birds.

Stock doves and squirrels were the first to find the boxes – but then last year the shadows returned; hunting, gliding, diving, talons striking from beneath silent wings. When death is silent we watch enchanted – 'haunting', 'beauty', 'nature', 'wonder' are the words we use. When death is noisy we watch horrified – 'cruel', 'disgusting', 'barbaric', 'ban it' are the words we think. How can death be banned? Eyes see the same process; minds see a different picture.

There were two nests last year and there are two nests this year too. Colin was apprehensive – were the boxes occupied; had they got young; was there enough food?

At the first box, he blocked the entrance hole; not only had it got four young – but both adults were inside too. He weighed the whole family – the male weighed 12 ounces. The young were small – vulture like – almost prehistoric and pot-bellied. They had fed well and there had been good hunting. As the young grow the male will leave the nest – returning only to feed the family. Bigger still

and more demanding – the female will seek daytime peace as well. Good hunting depends on cover and decent weather, not only for the owl, but for the mice and voles which are their victims.

Good news too at the second box – the adults had already been driven out by their demanding chicks, three were about to fledge and they were all heavier than the first male, weighing in at about 1 lb each. Owlets with puppy fat – they will lose weight before they fly.

It was going to be a butterfly day as well as an owl morning, but the rain came in like a gently rolling, falling mist. There would be no butterflies today; Colin rolled off with the mist – he will be back in a month to ring and record the four fluffy fatties.

When owls lay eggs, the female immediately begins to incubate. The first one to be laid is therefore the first to hatch. When butterflies lay eggs there is no hard and fast rule. With some they are laid in clumps, others are laid singly – some hatch quickly and the grub, larvae or caterpillar munches itself in to chrysalis, to emerge later with its own set of wings. Some remain eggs through autumn and winter and only hatch in the spring.

The eggs of the *large tortoiseshell* are laid on elm, sallow, willow and cherry in April and early May. They hatch after three weeks and munch into June. After a fortnight in a chrysalis – the butterfly emerges in July and that is when I saw a dozen – fresh and bright; one of Britain's most beautiful, extinct butterflies. Is it fair to include an 'extinct butterfly' in the Great British Butterfly Safari? Yes I did see the *large tortoiseshell*. It was not a fridge magnet or a broach – it was the real thing.

Cambridgeshire is almost lucky. It still has some old, moth eaten, just surviving elm spinneys. Dutch Elm Disease has struck, but some trees, shoots and suckers, survive. Branches die and fall off – but the trunks live on with a tight covering of leaves. To the *large tortoiseshell* butterfly the length of the branch is not important – all it needs are leaves for the caterpillars.

Bill had decided that there were enough leaves. 'Meet me by Long Bottom

Church at six', he said, 'and I will show you the *large tortoiseshell* butterfly – I've got a dozen just emerged.' He had hatched them; nurtured them and cosseted them in his garden and here they were in containers in the boot of his car. The rain had stopped but it was cloudy and overcast. Each one he took out lovingly with care, and placed it in elm scrub, sheltered by leaves in case of rain. One or two flickered their wings giving a fast flash of colour – but most kept their wings tightly closed to look exactly like elm bark.

Why the *large tortoiseshell* has become extinct in Britain no-one seems to know; climate change, parasites on the larvae, loss of elm or pollution, the final solution – who knows? Bill was simply doing his bit – he was sure the habitat was right; 'and with a little bit of luck…' I hope so. He spoke of owls and badgers, butterflies and flowers – an ordinary man with an ordinary job with an extraordinary love of nature. He looked up. The clouds were thickening and blackening; 'they'll be alright even if it rains' he said, 'they're butterflies'.

Tuesday July 9th

Today it was going to be the day of the *white admiral* – sun, blue sky, tall oaks, honeysuckle and the *white admiral* – a beautiful, beautiful butterfly. Instead it was cloud, rain, mud and wellington boots. Any admiral out today would be in charge of a submarine.

Wednesday July 10th

For years I never drew my bedroom curtains. With the dawn, sun or cloud, the arrival of light, accompanied by birdsong or snowflakes woke me – I then promptly fell asleep again.

Butterflies have interfered with this happy routine. The problem is that my days are too full; the Great British Butterfly Safari is one of the best, happiest and most educational undertakings of my life; but it has meant long hours travelling, searching, organising, celebrating, fretting, learning and laughing. I no longer want to wake with the dawn. I want to catch all the sleep I can get so I draw my curtains to retain the dark – I want a false dawn – to grab every extra hour of sleep I can.

I woke – switched the radio on, and oh what a surprise – 'After a bright early start – cloud and rain will be moving in from the west.' No lie-in today then – before the cloud comes I must try for the *white admiral* and one of the last *fritillaries* – the ***dark green fritillary*** – oh no – a notoriously fast flyer. I opened the curtains and sunlight burst in – the bright false dawn.

It was a day of bright false dawns – Brampton Wood, near Huntingdon – was almost perfect – a butterfly world – ***skippers***, ***Essex***, ***small*** and ***large***, ***ringlets***, ***meadow browns***, ***whites*** – ***large*** and ***small***, ***brimstones***, ***peacocks***, ***small tortoise-shells*** – but no ***white admiral***. 'Is this work?' Sarah asked. 'Of course it's work.'

Jet fighters arrived overhead – it was almost as if Brampton Wood was their marker for aerobatics training. The roars, screams and screeches were deafening – obscuring birdsong – I hope butterflies can shut out sound.

Clouds began to fill the sky from the west. We headed east at speed – abandoning all hope of ***white admirals***. It was a dash to the coast – a hurry to Holkham – ***dark green fritillaries*** love dunes, brambles and tufts of grasses. Despite girl-racer's best efforts, by the time we were in the dunes the clouds had arrived – the temperature dropped and even the nudists started putting on their clothes – another blank day.

Friday July 12th

To Welshpool and the Royal Oak. I have gone west – Sarah has gone south. I thought this would be a difficult, emotional day. Through Sarah's sunny disposition there is sadness and courage – her mother died when she was only seventeen – what a loss for a teenager. Now Simon's wife is dying suddenly and there seems no hope – so Sarah has headed for London.

When we came in May – Simon and Carol were happy – a brain tumour has appeared and unless there is a miracle (there was no miracle) nothing can be done. He is a brave man. 'Robin you must come – I want you to see my ***high brown fritillaries*** – Welsh ***high brown fritillaries*** – I want to show them to you.'

I wanted him to show me them – so here I was again at the Royal Oak. Simon and his daughter, Sophie, came and we went to the hospital where Carol was being cared for – there was recognition in her eyes and almost a smile – it would only be days – everybody sees that look sooner or later – to me it signifies the start of another journey – not the end – I am not a believer in random life, random creation, random nature, random universe. Mother, daughter, father, wife: there was love and emotion in that room – I left, I did not want to intrude. Life is so fleeting, so transient – for butterflies it is even more so – we must make the best of it – enjoy it – before it fades, flickers and disappears – if only there were no politicians to make our stay brighter.

We walked up towards the three butterfly moor. 'You don't know how I have been looking forward to this, Robin – it's so peaceful up here – after **high brown fritillaries** what are you after?'

'**Dark green** – I drew a blank two days ago.'

'We've got plenty here – while the sun shines we are bound to see them.' Can you believe it. I needn't have rushed to Norfolk after all.

The bracken was green and growing and yes, there were several **dark green fritillaries** flying fast and low over it. At an ooze of bog with sphagnum moss and marsh thistle on flower – **fritillaries** seemed to be everywhere – flying, gliding, drinking, feeding and mating. 'This is a very special place – we are probably looking at 25% of the Welsh population of the **high brown fritillary**.' Thank goodness – the last **fritillary** – I won't have to write it or spell it, after today.

Simon was amazing – spotting the difference between two very similar butterflies as they flew – 'there's a **dark green** – there's a **high brown** – spot the difference?' 'Just – if I use my imagination.' The **high brown** is normally associated with old native woodland – but they like the moor as both a source of nectar and food plant – the moor is one of the last places in Wales where the bracken is still harvested as bedding for cattle. When the bracken is cut it exposes the food plant below – violets. So the old 'inefficient' farming system benefits violets, butterflies and the farmers themselves – bracken costs nothing to grow whatsoever – to me that makes it an 'efficient' crop. Isn't it odd how economists and politicians steal and change the meaning of words? The other obvious theft is 'sustainable'; it is a word about nature, the environment, communities and the health of the planet – unscrupulous and ignorant politicians have corrupted it to include the circulation of money.

As we left the bog – two **dark greens** were still having a high time copulating on a marsh thistle flower – two butterflies locked in passion for three-quarters of an hour – looking in opposite directions – how do you tell if butterflies have their eyes shut? If too many people find out about the staying power of butterflies, I think the nectar of the marsh thistle could become extremely popular.

We walked through woods by a river, there was oak and mountain ash – the smell of bracken and sheep – the music of water over rocks with the occasional **high brown fritillary** almost floating and gliding in and out of shadow and sunlight.

It was a fine time – giving rest and recuperation – nature does not always heal – but it can help to restore.

Saturday July 13th

I was driving home along the M52. I had chosen the road as it usually has light traffic – I was thinking of Simon and Sophie. After I left them, I had spoken at a Countryside Alliance dinner on the edge of Wales, at a mini-country house – it seemed to go well.

I was lost in my thoughts – Jethro Tull was singing – yet again. I was cocooned – away from reality – what was I watching without its own sounds? Noiseless dust and metal flying through the air – red lights – rear brakes – a rolling lorry – fire – all to the music of Jethro Tull.

Suddenly the road was transformed into a war scene – still the cassette played – I had a windscreen-sized view of the world, surrounded by unreality. I stopped and flung open my door – reality – the smell of burning – the crackle of fire – people shouting and running. A juggernaught lorry had ploughed through the central reservation onto the opposite carriageway, turning over and ripping out a 100 yards of bent and jagged metal – the fat tattooed driver was lying on the side of the road – a car burned – with the driver inside – incinerated – there were people crying, phoning, dying – mayhem.

There was nothing anybody could do without skills – without equipment – the sheer helplessness of ordinary people in a high-tech disaster is as frightening as the disaster itself. Blue lights – yellow coats – people with skills and equipment – at least one person was beyond help. Returning to Eric was like returning to my cocoon, to safety – false safety. I drove around debris – and went on my way. I was lucky – 30 yards forward – I could have been caught by flying metal – 30 yards back and I could have been caught in the traffic queue – the road was closed for the rest of the day.

Jethro Tull was silent – two days – two tragedies – transience – what are we doing to butterflies, to air, to water, to our world, to ourselves? Onward and upward – forward for efficiency, technology to *progress*. Somewhere, somehow we have lost the plot – lost the point – why can't we take two paces backwards, pause, listen, look and think?

Through the gloom light – wings on the small box hedge near the farmhouse – one of my favourite butterflies – the first of the summer – the **gatekeeper**; orange-brown with a fringe of brown – a butterfly of sunny days and open wings – bramble blossom and blackberries – hedgerows – gateposts: it is the butterfly of harvest, sun and light – openings – farm gates – hence the name **gatekeeper**. There are always nature nerds and scientists who want to change things – to some the **gatekeeper** has become the '**hedge brown**', a butterfly much prettier than its new name. To me it will always be a butterfly of harvest, gateways, a picnic pause as harvest rests — it will always be the *gatekeeper*.

At dusk — more good news — Bill and Ben, again, what good men. They sounded conspiratorial — 'It's going to be fine tomorrow — meet us at ten and we will show you the *white letter hairstreak.*'

It was the end of another day; it had been the final end for some.

Sunday July 14th

The *white letter hairstreak* is another completely new butterfly to me. The *hairstreaks* — so far have been such unexpectedly beautiful butterflies — 'small is beautiful' — it has certainly been true with the *green hairstreak* and the *black hairstreak*. Not only is the *white letter hairstreak* in the same family as the *blues* and *coppers* — but it also has a strange link with ants — along with the caterpillars of the *silver-studded blue*, the *chalk hill blue* and the *green hairstreak* — not quite such a bizarre gastronomical link as the *large blue* — but still a link. The caterpillars have a honey gland on their bodies which secretes a fluid that ants seem to find as attractive as I find organic cider. As a result it is thought that the presence of ants deters predators such as bugs, wasps and flies. Sadly my presence near a bottle of organic cider does not seem to deter bugs, wasps and flies.

I met Bill and Ben at a field gateway not far from home — it was land owned by a government department. We skirted a field — walking between ripening wheat and a flowering hedge — already there were several *gatekeepers* and two were bonking. Bonking butterflies? No — that does not sound right.

Over a ditch and under a wire and we were in what remains of a small elm wood. At one time the dominant tree of Cambridgeshire was elm and there were numerous little elm woods and spinneys dotted all over the county. That was before the arrival of Dutch Elm Disease and the incompetence of bureaucrats, Eurocrats, local councillors and politicians that allowed it to spread with no action being taken.

This elm wood still has elms — but stunted elms: after the main passage of the disease, several trees and suckers survived — just — their branches died and fell off — but new leaves grow from long thin trunks. There are suckers with branches too — and every July the disease strikes some trees again, with the tell-tale signs of shrivelled and brown leaves giving a scorched appearance.

Bill was getting excited: 'This is a smashing little wood Robin — with the sun like this they will be flying.' We came to what was once a ride — now overgrown;

along its centre the grasses and thistles had been flattened. Bill went on; 'we do this every year – once the wood was managed for the *white-letter* – they don't bother now – so we try without them knowing. The trampling lets in light, and the butterflies love sunlight. What a government – it owns *white-letter hair-streaks* and doesn't help them – it's more concerned with what other people do to foxes.' If only Bill and Ben were in Parliament – their knowledge of the countryside, conservation and country people would shame the present 'prairie-brained Parliamentary spokespersons' on rural issues, but then it seems that the House of Commons is no longer a place where ordinary people either sit – or get represented. A 'prairie-brain' is a brain which stretches from the left ear to the right ear – but across which there are few signs of life or activity.

'Look on the thistle,' Bill whispered, 'a *white-letter hairstreak*'; it was another brown one and remarkably similar to the *black hairstreak* but with a different food plant – elm and wych elm instead of blackthorn. The 'hair' on each rear underwing shows a distinct W near rear orange patches and tail. To me 'rear orange patches and tail' sounds better than 'submarginal band of orange and black markings'.

The *white-letter* is another butterfly said to be hard to see but here they were easy – small and beautiful, feeding on thistles and brambles. Some settled on leaves – taking in sunlight, still with their wings closed. Others flew dizzily and distantly at tree-top height, where they settled and drank the 'honeydew' deposited on the leaves by aphids.

It was hot and getting hotter. I left Bill and Ben, as they were intending to visit several *white-letter* sites today – I had to move on to find out whether this heat would cause the *white admiral* to surface at last.

Sarah is back – she drove – tenant Tim was in the front passenger seat. He had never ridden with Sarah driving before – getting out at Brampton Wood he seemed quiet – verging on traumatised; he still talks about the experience.

A local expert had said '*they*' could be anywhere there is sun – but they should be around the large oaks in the main ride. '*They*' were. 'Look' said Tim, trauma vanishing, 'what a butterfly.'

What a butterfly indeed – dark velvet wings with a distinctive bright white band across the 2" wingspan. One flew twenty feet up – just below the canopy of oak – flying and gliding in and out of sun and shade – every time the sun hit its wings, the angles of light and gaze turned the wings into translucent silver. The good news is, that not only is the *white admiral* one of Britain's most beautiful butterflies – it is also one of the few that is increasing in numbers and

expanding its range. A reduction in woodland management has meant scruffier woods – if honeysuckle can be called scruffy. Honeysuckle is the food plant and in many woods it is no longer hacked and tidied – meaning more leaves on which munching caterpillars can feed; it also means more delicately scented summer evenings. More brambles also mean more nectar flowers for the adults, and along a smaller ride a butterfly flew low in front of me – obviously not a **rear admiral** – to land on a bramble flower .

The *flying time* of so many butterflies coincides with *bramble blossom* or does *flowering time* coincide with the *flying time* – which came first – the chicken or the egg; the butterfly or the blossom? The **white admiral** flies for a month – a whole month of added woodland beauty.

'We must fly Tim – we have to go to the Lakes tonight.'

Tim looked startled: 'Is Sarah going to drive?' 'Of course she is, some of the time.' It is a good job he is bald already otherwise, judging by his reaction, this revelation would have resulted in major stress and possible hair loss.

Back at Eric, Tim was attempting to look relaxed: 'Can I drive?' he tried to ask casually. I let him drive; the day had been far too good for anybody to have a nervous breakdown.

Monday July 15th – St Swithin's Day

A cooked breakfast in the Lakes – I needed energy and Ena's fried breakfast would provide it. But how would Sarah last – muesli and hot water, it was going to be a long, hard day.

St Swithin's Day is always important to me – if it rains – forty days of rain.

If it doesn't rain – forty days of fine weather – fine weather for harvest. It was cloudy – but the weather forecast was 'fine with sunny spells'. Today's desperately needed butterfly is another hit or miss butterfly – a high altitude butterfly – a butterfly that has chosen one of the wettest, cloudiest and coolest places to live – yet it will only fly in warm, sunny weather. This is not an Irish butterfly – it is not a **Paddy McMountain ringlet** – it is not found in Ireland at all; according to which book you read it is the **mountain ringlet**, or the **small mountain ringlet**.

The **small mountain ringlet** is apparently a remarkable butterfly. It is a smaller relative of the **Scotch argus** and they are both true alpine butterflies. I keep writing 'incredible' – but the **small mountain ringlet** is a survivor of the Ice Age with its origins in the Lakes going back 10,000 years – that really is *incredible*. Today it can only be found over 700 feet – oh no; if St Swithin is unkind then there will have to be a dash up to the Ben Nevis area of Scotland – where the flying time is slightly later.

Our guide is to be Simon Elliot – retired – a good man who I met several years ago, when he worked for English Nature.

Simon's stone house is near a stone church where he is a lay reader. Tall and thin he has the air of a monk, a mystic or an aesthete – or a mixture of all three; he lives simply and comfortably with a view and a dog.

Once in his little red car – all this changes. Does the hunched-up driving position of a tall man in a small car increase the blood pressure? Turn on the ignition and be becomes 'Boy Racer I', even faster than Booker and making Sarah look like a graduate of the School for Advanced Motoring. Tenant Tim – what would you do?

'Where did he go, Sarah? Can you see him?'

'He's vanished – open the window, see if we can smell burning rubber.'

The sun came out and went in. The clouds thinned over the crags – then thickened. We found One Aesthete and His Dog in the car park at Haweswater. It was a long, hard day. As time wore on Sarah's muesli and hot water had more staying power than my fry-up – but what had Simon and the dog been eating? Bonios and communion wine? They were inexhaustible.

At the butterfly site, among cotton grass, bog and mat grass close to where golden eagles sometimes try to breed, there was nothing. Cloud rolled in over the crags, the temperature dropped – we were well over 700 feet, more like 2,000 feet. Please St Swithin – don't let it rain – it didn't.

Sheep were on the hills having survived foot and mouth. The locals say that the sheep no longer say 'Baa, baa' they say 'Blair, Blair', remembering the name of the man who killed so many of their brothers, sisters and cousins during foot and mouth. I wonder if the Blair family has been vaccinated for protection against disease. If so why did they not allow the animals of the Lake District to be vaccinated?

I visited the Lakes at the height of foot and mouth – I saw sheep shot and left dead, piled high by the roadside for days on end. Cattle shot in the fields almost randomly and left lying where they fell. The sky was filled with the smoke of funeral pyres as animals were burned – I saw anger and tears – desperation and hopelessness.

Only one word comes to my mind when I think of it – *wickedness* – the *government* – the *politicians* who so love foxes and who dislike country people, carried out a policy of needless killing. Yet most of the animals were perfectly healthy – it was *wicked, ignorant, and heartless.* In many cases it was actually cruel. *Parliament* has *blood on it hands* and *hypocrisy in its heart.* As we trudged down we passed close to some sheep: 'Blair, Blair' they complained. I agreed.

Simon rushed off – 'See you in the morning' he said. The weather forecast for tomorrow is terrible – cloud and rain. We refuelled at *The Salutation*, a famous hunting pub at Threlkeld. Sarah's muesli and water was restored with a huge mound of meat, veg and wine – followed by pudding. Old friends David Grayling and his wife Ingrid were devouring similar portions – what had they done to build up such an appetite apart from selling antiquarian books, and run-ing a boarding home for dogs?

Mr Grayling tricked me and opened his wallet first. I swear a moth flew out. Moths have a variety of wonderfully descriptive names – but a moth Safari next year? With 2,500 species and most of them flying after dark – I don't think so – not even to see the inside of David Grayling's wallet again.

But David Grayling had one very good suggestion to make up for the blank day. 'All is not lost,' he said, 'imagine that you have seen a butterfly today – go and read a Lakeland poet – go and read William Wordsworth's *To a Butterfly* and a butterfly will fly into your mind.'

So I did just that:

> Stay near me – do not take thy flight
> A little longer stay in sight!
> Much converse do I find in thee,
> Historian of my infancy
> Float near me; do not yet depart!

Dead times revive in thee:
Thou bring'st, gay creature as thou art!
A solemn image to my heart,
My father's family.

Oh! pleasant, pleasant were the days,
The time, when in our childish plays,
My sister Emmeline and I
Together chased the butterfly!
A very hunter did I rush
Upon the prey: with leaps and springs
I followed on from brake to bush;
But she, God love her! feared to brush
The dust from off its wings.

Let's hope that tomorrow we have sunlight and more luck with the little gay creature.

Tuesday July 16th

Simon decided to try a different site – and as the weather forecast was bad, the sun shone brilliantly all day. We followed the distant red speck past the *Three Shires* pub and up into Wrynose Pass. What a beautiful wild place of bogs, crags, tarns and streams. I came here during the writing of *The Hunting Gene*; these are good, hard-working country people – a people with their own culture – a people who are misunderstood and where the villages, farms and way of life are viewed by some as simply the quaint ingredients of a rural theme park. A theme park entirely in place for the benefit of urban visitors. Unfortunately cultural cleansing and exploitation are evils that are not just limited to distant lands under political dictatorships.

We began our climb cautiously getting over an electric fence. Before foot and mouth, the local sheep knew their area – which crags, slopes and valleys were 'home-range' – they had been 'hefted on the hill'. Now new sheep with no ancestral memories of territory have to be 'hefted' artificially, helped by electric fences. It is a good idea, being pioneered by the National Trust – I hope it works.

Down is easy – down was easy – the sun was warm – Red Tarn was beautiful. Up is hard – up was very hard – steep and difficult – I was glad I had my crook.

We climbed almost to the top of Cold Pike – at nearly 2,259 feet. Sarah's breathing had hardly changed – she'll make Kilimanjaro easily later on in the year. My lungs were heavy and heaving – I'm determined to make it.

'Oh no – what do we do now?' the sun was out, the sky was blue, we were over 700 feet – everything was perfect – but where do we find the butterflies? The breeze was slightly cool, but there were outcrops of rock, depressions and hollows – all sun traps out of the wind, then there were patches of damp and bog – there were acres of it – just right for the **mountain ringlet** – but where do I start? I must think about it.

'Robin?' What does Sarah want now?

'Is this the butterfly you are looking for by my right boot?'

Lucky blue eyelashes – forget them – Sarah was wearing lucky walking boots and there – within two inches of her right foot – not a **mountain ringlet**, or even a **small mountain ringlet** – but the **very small mountain ringlet**. Evidently I had climbed 2,150 feet to see that tiny dark butterfly with deep dark red patches on its wings – just $1\frac{1}{2}$ inches across – am I sane? The small **mountain ringlet** is in fact very attractive – I think I am extraordinarily sane.

It flew fast and low, moth-like in a large half circle and as it went – other previously invisible **mountain ringlets** briefly flew up to it before disappearing again.

For the rest of the day it was all down hill. From the top of Cold Pike it was a warm stroll down to Eric and then at racing speed it was from highland – to lowland – to Meathrop Moss on the north side of Morecombe Bay. We passed a dirty lorry with graffiti: *A dog is for life; not just for Friday night*. And fancy that – graffiti with a semi-colon. What did it mean?

A northern 'Moss' is rather like a Cambridgeshire Fen. An undrained, unfarmed 'moss' becomes a raised 'Mire' or is it a lowland bog? Meathrop Moss is a bog – a flat bog – so boggy that the earth, or water, moves underfoot. Surrounded by birch and Scots pine it is an impressive bog and it was also a yellow bog – with hundreds of thousands of flowering bog asphodel. There were cranberry, rosemary and cross-leaved heath (heather), cottongrass and many large flopping butterflies, the **large heath**, lover of bogs and damp places, particularly in upland areas.

'While the sun's out – we must get on,' Simon urged. We were off again, the **large heath** safely ticked. Sarah was driving this time, trying to keep up with the little red car. With so many revs, changes in direction, dual carriageways and small country roads I had no idea where we were. We over took a car full of dogs – except for the driver – she looked very severe – did she start the day with a pint of vinegar? On the rear window was another dog slogan: *The more I see of men, the more I like dogs* – I don't understand that one either – shouldn't the middle word be 'women'?

Thank goodness for Simon – he had brought us to an old limestone quarry managed by the Cumbria Wildlife Trust, all we wanted now was the **northern brown argus**. The only difference between a **northern brown argus** and a **brown argus** – to a non **brown argus** is a tiny white spot on each fore-wing.

A warden was clearing invading brambles from an area of flower-filled grass. 'We are looking for the **northern brown argus**,' Simon told him. 'Oh', he said, 'you'll be lucky, I haven't seen one of those flying for a fortnight.'

So who has got it wrong? The books, the weather or the butterfly – doesn't the **northern brown argus** know when it's supposed to be flying? I couldn't believe it and in frustration I walked away through long grass leaving the others talking. Luckily impatient feet disturbed a little brown butterfly which flew and landed on an oxeye daisy – it opened its wings – two small white dots – the **northern brown argus** – the third and last of the three northern butterflies we had to see.

Thank you Simon – and there in the sunlight a miracle happened – I ceased to see him as a manic Michael Schumacher – instead he assumed the mantle of a modern day saint – St Francis of Assissi – aesthete – and finder of butterflies.

Thursday July 18th

The CRT's bid for Turnastone Court Farm in Herefordshire has been unsuccessful. Phew, what a relief – I can relax.

Friday July 19th

To Miriam's for lunch – just to talk butterflies. This Great British Butterfly Safari has taught me two things; Miriam Rothschild knows a great deal about butterflies and I know very little.

Ashton Wold was looking quiet and peaceful under the sun – it would do, as I was not intending to see butterflies today; the sun was shining and there was little wind.

At the age of 24, Miriam's father cycled from Cambridge to Ashton and went looking for butterflies – he was so impressed that he decided he would like to buy it. He asked a local who owned it. 'The most eccentric man in England, if not Europe,' came the reply, 'Lord Rothschild.' So he did not have to buy it after all – his father owned it already, as a payment for bad debts.

At 94, Miriam still loves the place – although butterfly numbers have plummeted despite all her care. Several **fritillaries**, the **Duke of Burgundy fritillary** and the **chequered skipper** have all vanished from Ashton Wold.

She gained her love of butterflies from her father. When she was under five she took a **comma** to him and said: 'This isn't a **tortoiseshell,** what is it?' I didn't discover the difference until I was forty-five – I think that adequately describes the intellectual gap between us. Her father died when she was fifteen – it upset her so much that she abandoned butterflies for two years.

She is baffled why some of Ashton's butterflies have gone. She suspects the cause is spray drift or residues from farming chemicals. For ten years she tried farming organically, but Ministry tests revealed that the changes made little difference to the levels of chemical traces around the estate. She believes that butterflies are important for many reasons. As significant as any is their beauty and the aesthetic pleasure they can give – only yesterday she saw a group of smiling people watching a **purple emperor** sitting in the road, flapping its wings in the sunlight. That reminds me – **purple emperor –** I must try and see that soon – it could be difficult if the weather changes.

She believes that butterflies are important for introducing children to wildlife and getting them interested. Then there is science – the breeding, the genetics, even antibiotics are being found in butterflies and all could be important in the

future. Lunch was also important and at the table Miriam told me of her concern
for flies as well as butterflies. How Ashton Wold's fly population has tumbled and
so have the numbers of swallows and house martins, possibly as a direct result.
'Why only yesterday,' she said, 'a fruit fly landed on a banana I was about to eat –
I was so pleased to see it, I let it have the banana.'

The policy was being very successful. I went over to finish the meal with
fresh raspberries. A cloud of at least 150 fruit flies took off. I was less kind than
Miriam – I denied them a good helping. She is always an inspiration; she has
been so supportive of the CRT – giving us advice, encouragement and her hay
meadow mixtures have been a complete success.

I travelled from sanity to insanity; Ashton Wold to the A14. Friday afternoon
and already east/west traffic from Cambridge to Huntingdon was almost stationary. Right on cue for the 470th time Simon and Garfunkel sang:

> 'I long to be homeward bound
> I wish I was homeward bound.'

How those stationary, over-heating, poet's day drivers and commuters would
have agreed. How glad I was to be travelling west/east. The radio offered no
comfort. That wonderful intellectual John Prescott has announced plans for
50,000 more houses for the Cambridge area – I wonder how many additional
cars they will generate? He surely is to the environment what the Sahara Desert
is to skiing: what Mike Tyson is to flower arranging; what Attila the Hun was to
World Peace; what Tony Blair is to Statesmanship; what Osama bin Laden is to
the Christian Evangelical Alliance and what DDT is to butterflies. That is my
opinion anyway – if he came to the farm I wouldn't let him near the cows in
case they caught something and I wouldn't even allow my sister Rachael's dog
near him in case Jonah got bitten. Phew – that feels better.

The environmental illiteracy of all the hundreds of thousands of houses proposed for the south-east is beyond belief. Britain's population is only growing at
the rate of 0.18% a year which means that what is happening is caused by the
government simply moving people to jobs instead of jobs to people. While some
northern towns empty and crumble – southern towns expand and burst. So the
mistakes made during the industrial revolution are being repeated during the
technological revolution.

As usual insidious, mindless spin surrounds the whole thing. The advance of
Fatty Prescott's concrete jungle is being masked by the *political word thieves* who

are referring to the 'Sustainable Communities Plan'. Real communities develop for a variety of reasons, trade, travel or because of the physical features of the land – they continue developing as communities, mixing antiquity, stability and continuity. Prescott's 'communities' will be neither communities nor sustainable, they will only be developed for reasons of greed, expediency and short-term politics – not a very good excuse for ripping the heart out of the English countryside.

Prescott has ruined a good day. My local post office hasn't helped matters either; it is selling 'English eating apples – Vista Bella 88p kg'. How can English apples be called Vista Bella – and surely English apples are sold by the pound?

Rachael has made things even worse. She has produced a jar of 'English Honey' – large print, packed in Wales – small print. And now it's the turn of cricket – on the radio. The commentator – 'Blowers' has some bottled water – he tells us the label reads 'pure mountain water – percolating through the Pyrenees for a 1,000 years' – then best of all – 'sell-by date August 23rd'.

The whole world is going mad except me and Miriam Rothschild.

Monday July 22nd

Purple hairstreaks are flying – back to the A14 – Huntingdon and Brampton Wood. All you have to do apparently is to look at the right oak tree. I'm sure it will be beautiful like all the other **hairstreaks**.

'Sarah – there!'

'Where?'

'There.'

'It's not.'

'There it is again – look!'

'Robin – there.'

'Where?'

'There!'

'It's not.'

'There it is again – look.'

A monosyllabic butterfly conversation can be very brief, but it is the only sort of conversation possible to accompany the sighting of *purple hairstreaks*. The *purple hairstreak* butterfly flies so quickly and so briefly – at the top of tall oak trees; it's a case of 'now you see it, now you don't'. But we've seen it – just.

Tuesday July 23rd

Chris Knights knows of *purple hairstreaks* in Norfolk. 'You can see them easily in trees next to an old railway line – come over.' So I had the same conversation with Chris today that I had with Sarah yesterday.

'Robin – there!'

'Where?'

'There.'

'It's not' – and vice versa.

'Well they were *purple hairstreaks*,' Chris said defensively.

'Have you photographed them, Chris?'

'No, they move too fast – can you describe them to me, Robin?'

'No, they move too fast – but we have seen them.'

'Yes and you've seen them two days running – don't write too much about them, you'll run out of paper.'

Wednesday July 24th

In theory the *purple emperor* can be seen in July and August. In practice it is one of Britain's rarest and most elusive butterflies. Originally I had planned to go to Oxfordshire, Wiltshire or even the New Forest to try and search it out – but if

Miriam says it is currently flying in Northamptonshire – I will try Northamptonshire – it will save time and fuel.

My only sighting of the ***purple emperor*** in the past was in Northamptonshire – when I went to the wood made famous by the late Denys Watkins-Pitchford who wrote beautiful children's books and countryside books under the name of BB. BB lived in a remarkable round house – an old toll house on the road from Thrapston to Corby. Along a country road and up a hill, his local wood seemed the ideal place for ***purple emperors*** – containing tall oaks, where the butterflies spend much time, high up in the canopy, and sallow – the food plant. The wood is a large wood and stretches to the land of Miriam Rothschild, and it was there that he decided to introduce his beloved butterfly.

His scheme was successful – his carefully bred and released ***purple emperors*** survived and flourished. He was an old-style traditional country gentleman – he taught art at Rugby school, fished and shot, indeed his *nom de plume* BB is a type of wildfowling cartridge; he painted, drew, and used scraper board – his writing was lyrical and beautiful – verging on poetry. I met him with my hyper-active hedge-laying friend Badger Walker – and together we went egg collecting. We went collecting the eggs of ***purple emperors***. Each year after he had introduced the butterfly to his wood, he returned to collect some of their eggs, laid singly on the upper surface of sallow leaves. As his old eyes faded – Badger became his searcher and finder. Once collected, he watched over the eggs in his garden – through all the stages of life, until the butterflies emerged the following July, when he would release them back into his butterfly wood.

Every one of his 59 books started with a woodcut of a cowslip and the lines:

> The wonder of the world
> The beauty and the power
> The shape of things,
> Their colours, lights and shades,
> These I saw.
> Look ye also while life lasts.

Life doesn't last and BB died in 1990, but Badger had heard that twelve years later the butterflies were still alive and well and living in the wood. Two years ago I went in search of the ***purple emperor*** in BB's wood – with Badger and the beautiful foxhound pup I was walking at the time – Corset – but we saw no

urban vandals of the House of Commons. How can the will of an urban majority be called 'democracy' when it is imposed on a rural minority? Let the towns look after themselves and the country look after the country. What we have now is not democracy but domination and intimidation – one group dominating another.

The **chalkhill blues** are glad of the earlier invasions. Most of Cambridgeshire's chalk land has been ploughed and cultivated – giving no rest and recreation to **chalkhill blues**. But Devil's Dyke provides this long thin hill of grasses and wildflowers that thrive on chalk – there are harebells, scabious and stemless thistles, clover, knapweed and white eyebright. There are vetches too, including horseshoe vetch – the only food plant of the caterpillar of the **chalkhill blue**. And there are butterflies – all of July's common butterflies seemed to be welcoming the sun – making up for lost time – feeding, fighting, coupling, and absorbing the sun through open wings. The **chalkhill blue** is the second largest blue butterfly (second equal with the **adonis blue**) but unlike some of the others it is instantly recognisable to the layman's eye, being a light, silvery blue. They were everywhere – blue jewels almost dancing through the blue heads of harebells and scabious – a happy blue – a summer blue – a blue of flowers, grasses and open spaces – a blue from the past that has brought distant memories to the present – memories of a time when the land was more than just a food factory, a development site and place to build a motorway.

AUGUST

Friday August 2nd

A dawn with more blue than grey, more open sky than cloud – I have made the decision – I will go to Dorset, or more precisely, I will go to Lulworth Cove. It sounds a good idea – Dorset is always a fine place to go – wet, windy or sunny: autumn, summer or winter – but oh no, it is also Friday – meaning jammed motorways – mile after mile of over-heating, almost stationary metal – engines revving – gases rising – petrol pumping – tills ringing and revenue falling into the Chancellor of the Exchequer's tax money box, as if he has won the Lottery. Long-term global warming: long-term climate change: long-term sea level rise: long-term calamity? Who cares when you are a short-term politician in an unscrupulous government with little interest in the air we breathe, or the greenhouse gases we generate. To the political mind the great car economy equals tranquillity and green pastures. To tranquillity and green pastures the great car economy equals melting ice caps and deep-sea diving suits.

It is peak holiday time too, so that Poet's Day – 'P... Off Early, Tomorrow's Saturday' – will be made worse by all those happy families in overcrowded cars going off on their fortnight of frolicking and falling out by the sea.

The Great British Butterfly Safari is gradually turning Sarah into a butterfly – not a nine to five butterfly – but a real butterfly – waiting for the sun from 6am to 6pm – not Monday to Friday – but Sunday to Sunday. Just like the **purple emperor** she flits here and there, needing to re-charge her urban batteries from time to time. She manages like the **purple emperor**, by visiting various deposits, especially that large steamy deposit around the Thames. As a result she has opted for the lure of London this weekend, rather than the allure of Lulworth Cove – which is a problem. I don't want another **purple emperor** pageant, with no witnesses, when the Dorset butterflies appear. When the legion of **Lulworth skippers** skip into view – or a cloud of migrating **monarchs** come in off the sea – the Great British Butterfly Safari must be accompanied by belief rather than disbelief, and reality rather than unreality. I don't want my credibility to sink to the same level as that of the Chancellor of the Exchequer – consequently I need someone to accompany me to darkest Dorset – the home of naked giants and car thieves.

How I thanked the wet week, for I found an instant replacement butterfly adjudicator – not with smiles, blue eyelashes, and red toenails, sadly – but with a long face, bald head and hairy legs. Tim, the tenant of Lark Rise Farm, was getting depressed with the wet and the halt in his harvest – a day's butterflying would do him good.

It was an extraordinary start to the day with traffic moving on the M25, the M3 and the M27; there must be a catch somewhere. Ringwood in two and a quarter hours and still no catch – in fact quite the reverse – with the few remaining clouds melting away and the sky becoming a cloudless blue.

Despite the naked giants and furtive thieves, Dorset is still a wonderful county – no wonder Gordon Beningfield loved to paint it in watercolours and Thomas Hardy re-created it in words. Even now, despite the efforts of Europe and second-rate politicians Dorset can still be recognised as Dorset, and not as a homogenised, sanitised province of Greater Euroland – the social arm of Euro Disney!

Around every corner there are scenes that Gordon would have wanted to put onto canvas, or a picturesque village or farm that Hardy would have washed with tears. Gordon's pictures were celebrations; Hardy's stories were disintegrations – communities, families and lovers, all falling apart, and all inspired by the same beautiful, haunting, harrowing landscapes – woods, heaths, downs, coombes, meadows, marshes, cliffs, sand, sea, pebbles, cottages, cattle, flowers, birds and butterflies. Even such *landscapes* cannot reproduce sounds and scents – and if there are 'downs' why not 'ups' – *skyscapes*?

Butterfly Conservation is a lucky organisation to be housed in a modernised Dorset farmyard in the butterfly capital of Britain. It is the pub capital too, and as we sat in the garden of the *Weld Arms* the talk was of food and butterflies, and butterflies as food. Did Martin Warren have to talk about butterfly wings while I was eating quiche – full of sweetcorn – quiche rather than a butterfly steak? It always strikes me as being a total waste of time and energy eating sweetcorn – it seems to leave the body in the same state as it enters it – even **purple emperors** would have trouble recycling once eaten sweetcorn.

Perhaps that is why birds and mice don't eat butterfly wings – indigestion or non-digestion – they are the sweetcorn of wild food. Flycatchers won't eat them – they discard them, mice won't eat them, they discard them, and even wrens won't eat them. The body, yes, is devoured happily but the wings of butterflies

always get thrown away like burger cartons. Martin had a jar of wings – guess the number and divide by two – that gives the number of butterflies murdered during their hibernation in his garden shed; butterflies are so easy to eat for a mouse, during hibernation. A vegetarian colleague could match it – he had a cluster of eighteen **peacock** butterflies in a huddle of hibernation in his shed. Then – one morning he found thirty-six wings – they had been found – not by mice, but non-vegetarian wrens – little Jenny Wren – one minute singing sweetly to cheer up winter – the next scoffing butterflies. Oh dear – hunting wrens – and to make the matter worse, I'm sure they enjoyed it.

Oh no – how, in the course of one quiche, can the conversation become so indigestible. Butterflies… **wood white** willies – yes insect genitalia over lunch/ dinner. What is even worse – apparently – is that the study of insect genitalia, to find new species, is not just a matter of willie-watching with magnifying glasses – it involves dissection of the assorted parts in question. Does this mean lancing the loins of the **Lulworth skipper** to find **LULWORTH SKIPPER TWO**? I hope not. And what about *Homo sapiens* – are all the private parts of people to be studied in detail, to find new species and sub-species? That would turn the race-relations industry into a spectacular spin. If science is good enough for butterflies then it should be good enough for people, but if science is too bad for people then surely it should also be too bad for butterflies!

Martin has been a real star during the Great British Butterfly Safari – telling me when, where, and how to see butterflies. He continued at Lulworth Cove, in its chocolate-box setting. Gordon Beningfield's paintings are sometimes described unflatteringly as 'chocolate-boxy'. How can beautiful places and things be painted honestly, in a way not to appeal to chocolate-box makers?

Immediately we walked into long grass at the edge of Lulworth Cove, Martin showed me when, where and how to see butterflies. 'There's a *chalkhill blue*,' he said enthusiastically after one second. So I needn't have rushed off to Newmarket in a state of near hysteria. 'There's a *clouded yellow*,' he said enthusiastically after two seconds. What a relief – early indications were that it was going to be a bad *clouded yellow* year. 'There's a *Lulworth skipper*,' he said enthusiastically after three seconds. Really! Had I come all this way to see that small brown butterfly – the *dullworth skipper* surely? 'There's a *marbled white*,' he said enthusiastically after four seconds. After eight seconds we had seen eight species. Tim looked at Martin – here was a man who knew his stuff. Tim looked at me – here was a man who ate vegetarian quiche.

The sun shone – the sea was calm and Martin hunted for butterflies. Here was grass eaten by the *Lulworth skipper*; there were more *clouded yellows* and 'look at that view': incredible – an 'expert', looking beyond his expertise – a rarity indeed.

The *clouded yellows* were wonderful – flying fast – here, settling there – the sun catching their bright sulphur wings. Martin had to return to his desk: sadly in a world of pens and paper, emails and information – desk management becomes as important as butterfly management. How lucky are butterflies! They can float on the breeze, settle on flowers and bask in the sun – while others send emails to manage them.

Tim met a butterfly with brown, laughing eyes and a mobile phone and walked into Lulworth Cove to sit on the pebble-strewn beach. Days off require discomfort, classed as outdoor enjoyment. I stayed on to watch the *Lulworth skipper*. It lives for twenty miles along the Dorset coast – the only place in Britain. Global warming and greenhouse gases will help it spread: perhaps the Chancellor of the Exchequer is a conservationist after all, with a particular love for the *Lulworth – dullworth skipper*.

I hadn't been on a British beach during holiday time for years. How would I find Tim and the brown-eyed butterfly among all those bodies – most of them like butterflies trying to absorb the sun?

There were old men wearing baseball caps backwards, trying to look young; young boys smoking cigarettes frontwards, trying to look old; fat people bulging out of brief holiday wear trying to look thin and the thin people keeping most of their clothes on to give the impression of the perfect body. One woman turning pink in her bikini looked like a beached seal – she tried to shift her bouncing buttocks to get the other side pink.

Where bodies were brown – the browner the body, the greater the area of exposure – the briefer the top and the briefer the bottom. In the case of the displaying males – then the larger the bottom, the briefer the shorts and the greater the stomach overhang. I was thankful that they were not butterflies, that their genitals were covered, and that there were no scientists undertaking species research.

With the **dullworth skipper** and the **clouded yellow** duly ticked – there was a chance of one more butterfly – the **silver-spotted skipper** – a lover of short, grazed grass – not cliff tops and the smell of sea.

The **silver-spotted skipper** is a butterfly of August – but we might still be one or two days early. We drove the short journey to Fontwell Down; what a place and what a view – a steep sided valley-coombe bathed in evening sunlight – there were **skippers** – **large**, **small** and **Essex**, there were **small heaths**, **ringlets**, **meadow browns**, **gatekeepers**, **common blues** and **chalkhill blues**. Another butterfly twitcher approached; 'Is this the right place for the **silver-spotted skipper**?' I had no idea before the Great British Butterfly Safari that there were butterfly twitchers – there were – there are.

Alas, we walked down the down, along the down and up the down, but the **silver-spotted skippers** were not to be spotted. Who cares: it was just a pleasure to be in Hardy Country; to be part of a Beningfield landscape.

Sunday August 4th

Oh no: it's grey, it's raining – I am supposed to be going west again to Wayills Boyo. I want to go – but not another long drive in the rain – the chances of seeing any of the remaining butterflies are nil, unless the **silver-spotted skipper** has become the rain-spotted **skipper**.

It is the day of Henry's *Revolting Peasants' Party* at Usk Castle. I want to go – I would meet the Wurzels – the musical highlight of my life – at last the Wurzels. I looked out of the window at the great grey covering of cloud; at the rain hitting my window pane – I rolled over and went to sleep again. I dreamt of wurzels – sadly they were mangold wurzels and were eaten by cows.

Monday August 5th

Oh no: a phone call from Sarah in her car again. She is not lost: the rust bucket has broken down in the middle carriageway of the M11. What should she do? The obvious answer is – get rid of the rust bucket. It sounds a nightmare. I suggested she tried to get to the side of the motorway and then to the nearest motorway service station.

Twenty minutes later, another phone call from Sarah – she sounds traumatised. She has managed to escape from the rust bucket and two drivers stuck behind her have helped her push it to the side. When a butterfly dies it quickly gets eaten – or simply disappears – if only old Fords were the same as butterflies. She tells me that one of the drivers will take her to the service station near Stansted.

Twenty-five minutes later I arrive at the service station. I really needed a boat – not Eric the Freelander. Yet another thunderstorm swamped the road and the fields – the stuttering harvest is still stuttering. At last the music of the Jethro Tull was appropriate – 102 plays later – August Rain.

Sarah appeared – she looked traumatised: it is not the fault of the butterflies that the Ford rust bucket is not up to a weekly migration to and from the Black Hole. It is one of the oddities of butterflies that our most rare and beautiful butterfly is named after one of the dingiest and dirtiest parts of the Black Hole – London. Even the dingiest *dingy skipper* does not deserve to be named after an area of London – but the *Camberwell beauty* was – and is.

It is apparently a sensational butterfly; velvet maroon – or chocolate brown – depending on which book is read – with blue spots and cream edges to its wings. The wingspan is about $2\frac{1}{2}$ inches – big enough to fly it from Scandinavia and Germany – I wonder how many break down on the way? Why it does not stay here, breed here and thrive here is a mystery – its food plants are willow, sallow, elm and birch. The first British *Camberwell beauty* was named in Camberwell in 1748. It was seen two miles south of London Bridge: it is attracted to water and willow trees and at that time the Thames had abundant willows and its largest tributary was not a sewage treatment works as it is today.

So the *Camberwell beauty* is a migrant – a vagrant. It is one of the few things that I have in common with the *Camberwell beauty* – that as a young writer with no money, I too became a vagrant for a few weeks in order to write – with no expenses. My last port of call was also Camberwell – Camberwell Reception Centre – then still run like a Victorian Work House with tramps, drunks, dossers, lunatics and ne'er-do-wells. Almost the only anti-social group missing from that collection of misfits was politicians. There was dirt, squalor, louse parades, fights and little of beauty. How the appearance of a *Camberwell beauty* would have raised the spirit.

Somehow I had to raise the spirits of a Hammersmith Beauty, whose fluttering days appeared to have crash landed in the middle of the M11. What is worse, the Ford rust bucket had behaved just like a butterfly: a circuit of the motorway where it had died revealed that it had completely disappeared.

Alas, without her knowledge, Sarah's car had died in an area of 'road works' with 'free recovery' operating. The dreadful car had been 'recovered' – oh no! It took Sarah some time to recover and she decided that she needed longer migrations back to London, to earn more money one or two days a week and breathe in again the scents and sounds of Hammersmith High Street.

I wrote her a job reference – with three butterflies to go – perhaps the Great British Butterfly Safari could be downgraded to the Not So Great British Butterfly Safari and operate just three days a week.

Wednesday August 7th

Oh dear: the reference was too good and Sarah has been offered a full-time job already in the Black Hole – starting on Monday. It is still raining – with three butterflies to go – the **silver-spotted skipper**, the **brown hairstreak** and the **Scotch argus** – there is little likelihood that the sun will shine and wings will fly before Sarah returns to nine to five – instead of dawn to dusk.

However, would the rust bucket be in a condition to return her to Hammersmith High Street? We located it in a 'pound' under a flight path to Stansted Airport. I had heard of a 'pound' for dogs before – but never dead cars. Sarah sat in it – turned the key, and much to her embarrassment the engine burst into instant life. Why can't butterflies have lives that last as long as old Ford cars? Butterflies are far more beautiful: they travel quietly and when in a collision they do far less damage.

Sunday August 11th

It rained in the morning: St Swithin I hate you. At this rate with all this water about the **silver-spotted skipper** is in danger of becoming the **silt-splattered skipper**. Of course each of the three remaining butterflies will only fly in direct sunlight and the **skipper** and the **hairstreak** have very brief lives. The **silver-spotted skipper** flies for only two weeks and the **brown hairstreak** lives

for only three weeks as a butterfly. With the **Scotch argus** things are slightly better and it can be seen in July and August – if it stops raining will I see them?

In the afternoon it stopped raining and the sun put in a fleeting appearance – I hope the butterflies woke up long enough to see it.

Monday August 12th

The sun is still shining and it is the Glorious Twelfth – grouse shooting starts. I wonder if Alun Michael has appeared on a grouse moor with gun in hand, knees in tweed and dog at heel – to show his loyalty to his new found love – shooting? As an urban Labour minister I wonder if he would shoot butterflies – perhaps the government could give grants for specially trained dogs to flush out the **cabbage white** so that it can be peppered by guns loaded with miniature shot – butterfly balls – not mothballs – with the shooters concealed behind rows of sprouting broccoli.

I wonder if Alun Michael knows the difference between a grouse and a **cab-bage white** butterfly? I do wonder a lot about Alun Michael. I wonder who will remember his name, two days after he retires from Parliament? I wonder if Alun Michael will remember his own name two days after he retires from Parliament?

Oh dear – there are even worse things to consider than Alun Michael. In came three phone calls – all three informed me that butterflies have been flying today in different parts of the country – the **Scotch argus** in the Lake District, the **brown hairstreak** in Oxfordshire and the **silver-spotted skipper** at Porton Down – PORTON DOWN? How do I get into Porton Down? It means a week in prospect of miles, mayhem and praying for the sun.

Tuesday August 13th

Off to Porton Down. The radio tells me it is 'International Left Handers Day' – oh dear. Left handers feel left out – discriminated against – so we need a special day. How have all those left-handed international cricketers managed I wonder – and all those left-footed football players? I want to start an 'Irritated By Politicians Day'. When all our politicians have to spend a day doing a real job – serving us – waiters, road sweepers, dustmen – a total novelty to most of them. After such an experience would they want the rest of the year off – so it's back to being politicians again then!

Just along the road, a sign was advertising a local pub – then came another sign, 'oops missed it'; a flattened pigeon on the road next to it hadn't been missed. At this time of year the wildlife corpses on our roads show how the average driver simply doesn't care about, or understand, the countryside being driven through. It reminded me of a day in May when I showed Sarah a young mistle thrush in the garden. It flapped off and landed in the middle of the road, quietly minding its own business. It was a mistake. With at least one hundred yards, in which to slow, stop or even get out in a 30mph speed limit and move the little bird – a large, black, shiny, posh car came along and flattened the fledgling. Never mind – we must ban fox hunting – it is cruel – but please don't mention Muslim halal slaughter or the 250 million creatures killed on our roads every year.

As Porton Down drew nearer – I saw a feature I had never noticed before – wild yew trees growing singly and in clumps along the hedgerows. The yew is a most attractive evergreen tree – but it is deadly poisonous to livestock. How did the old shepherds and cattle drovers keep their animals away from freely growing yew and how long does it take roe deer to learn not to take the occasional mouthful? Quite unsurprisingly no butterfly has yew as its food plant.

Porton Down itself is one of the most sensitive sites in Britain. It is sensitive – I assume – because if you are a dusky Arab in a white coat playing with chemical and biological research you are said to be a 'terrorist' developing weapons of 'mass destruction'. If you are British or American – wearing a white coat and playing with chemical and biological research you are said to be a 'scientist' working to save us from weapons of mass destruction. If you are doing this work in Britain, you are probably doing it at Porton Down. So not only is Porton Down highly sensitive – it also has high security for the whole of its 7,000 acres.

Land that is highly sensitive, with high security, is very good for highly sensitive, insecure butterflies – with the *silver-spotted skipper* being particularly sensitive and insecure. It flourishes on Porton Down – safe from developers, airport planners, ploughs, combine harvesters, agricultural chemicals and John Prescott. What other chemicals are at Porton Down is anybody's guess – but at least there are rolling acres of fenced off downland ideal for *skippers*, *jumpers*, *floppers*, *fliers* and *blues*.

The man who had come to my *silver-spotted skipper* rescue was a Wiltshire farmer with a small colony of '*silver-spots*' on his land. 'I can't guarantee them', he said, 'but there are thousands on Porton Down', and Porton Down had agreed to show me some of their thousands.

I met Fred Fieldgate in *The Pheasant Pub*, an old coaching inn along the A30. I had been there – and Porton Down – years before, to see an experiment to bring back the Great Bustard to Salisbury Plain. It had failed, and so the Great Bustard, then extinct in Britain, is still extinct in Britain. I hope those rotten Bustards had not been eating *silver-spotted skippers*.

Fred Fieldgate was not christened Fred Fieldgate – it was his pen name for a local Wiltshire newspaper. Fred Fieldgate? I suppose it is slightly better than Earnest Spreader or Bert Hedgelayer. I suppose too that a young modern farming writer would choose Gary Sprayer or Simon Subsidy.

Fred Fieldgate was until recently a tenant farmer – now he is a retired tenant farmer spending his time managing a chunk of retained downland for sheep and wildlife. Of course at the same time he has to fight that major scourge of farming and *countrylife* – the *lowlife* Labour government.

The approaches to Porton Down were interesting – sheep and cattle? There is a persistent rumour that the great foot and mouth epidemic of 2001 was started by experiments in the north of England using live foot and mouth virus from either Porton Down, or the Veterinary Investigation Centre at Pirbright. Without a Public Enquiry we will never know the truth and the government will not allow a Public Enquiry. These are the same politicians who – when in opposition – were nearly all in favour of a 'Freedom of Information Bill'. 'Freedom of Information', it would seem, is only an option when you have no information.

If foot and mouth did start with live virus experiments which got out of control, then the compensation claims against the government would be astronomical. No wonder the nice Mr Blair wants no Public Enquiry – freedom of information on foot and mouth obviously might lead to foot in mouth.

The different, fenced-off blocks, containing laboratories inside Porton Down look sinister. The cameras in the reception at Porton Down are more sinister. 'Turn round – look up and smile at the camera' the receptionist ordered. I turned round, looked up and smiled at the camera; almost immediately my picture was printed onto my pass on her desk – clever that – she smiled. She looked normal – one head – two hands and she was the colour of fake tan – not green or throbbing blue.

A notice informed 'Today's Research – Tomorrow's Health'. I looked for one saying 'Today's Cliché – Tomorrow's Lie'. It is obviously still at the printers.

As we waited for our escorts a very dusky gentleman arrived of Arab appearance. An Iraqi at Porton Down must be as rare as a *silver-spotted skipper* in the middle of the M25.

Fred was impressed – our escort turned out to be two escorts. A military conservationist and a female, RSPB, stone curlew counter – it must be wonderful counting stone curlews for a living: I have certainly enjoyed my summer of counting butterflies.

Porton Down – away from the files, the microscopes and the foot and mouth virus was a wonderful place – old ancient downland looking new and pristine. It has to look new – there is so little of it – but it is a system of plants, animals and butterflies that goes back into history – to shepherds and sheep, cottages, villagers, W. H. Hudson and a way of life that has disappeared in its entirety; apart from this old wild place surrounded by fences and security cameras.

Lowland heath – of grasses and wildflowers – the call of stone curlews, the song of larks and the wings of butterflies – hundreds of them – clouds of them – butterflies, *meadow browns*, *small tortoiseshells*, *brimstones*, *peacocks*, *whites* – *large* and *small*, *gatekeepers* – wings, sunlight, grasses, the dappled light of woodland edge, more wings, and another cloud of butterflies. There are people who claim that 'clouds of butterflies', 'armfuls of wildflowers' are the romantic memories of childhood exaggerated by time, imagination, dreams and wishful thinking. The clouds of butterflies at Porton Down show that the dreamers have dreams based on reality, not on short memories, dulled vision and stunted lives.

'What's that?' I asked, 'Juniper?'. It was acres of rolling lowland juniper. I had heard of a 'gin clear' water before – but not 'gin sweet' air.

In a gentle valley of sun-bleached grasses, thistles, wild basil and clumps of blackthorn we stopped. Miss Stone-Curlew-Counter was 'into' butterflies too: 'I saw a *brown hairstreak* here this morning' she said casually. I couldn't believe my ears. The *brown hairstreak* was going to be my hardest butterfly I had been told – harder even than the *very small mountain ringlet*. Apparently the *brown hairstreak* spends most of its life either doing very little at the top of tall trees: or doing very little at the bottom of thick hedges or clumps of scrub.

'*Brown hairstreak*?' – I couldn't believe my ears.

'Yes' she said, 'it was feeding on the flower of a thistle.'

Close to the Land Rover was a flowering thistle; on the thistle flower was a butterfly – a brown butterfly – a *BROWN HAIRSTREAK* – I was amazed, astonished – guess what – the **BROWN HAIRSTREAK** was actually BROWN – but a very distinctive, attractive brown. Here was 'the most difficult butterfly' – not in the distance – high or low, but two feet away and looking huge through my trusty monocular. What a beautiful butterfly. What beautiful additions to my life the *hairstreak* butterflies have been – how have I been indifferent to such beautiful, delicate creatures for so long? It was in perfect condition – with closed wings, rich in shades of copper and brown, with streaks of white and an orange tail. The mixture of surprise and beauty literally took my breath away – here was number fifty-six; I was ahead of schedule.

The only food plant of the *brown hairstreak* is blackthorn – while the adults feed on aphid honeydew and nectar from fleabane, thistle flowers and bramble. It is now one of Britain's rarest and most localised butterflies. Miles of blackthorn hedgerow and acres of blackthorn scrub have gone from the countryside – tidied, cultivated, 'rationalised'.

With them no doubt has gone the *brown hairstreak* – from unobtrusive commoner – to almost vanished rarity. As all those clumps of blackthorn were removed from my own parish – did the *brown hairstreak* disappear with them? I will never know. Being a late flying butterfly, the *brown hairstreak* lays its eggs singly on twigs of blackthorn and they do not hatch until the following May, by which time the white blossom of the blackthorn winter has turned into the tender green of new spring leaves.

'Look here', shouted Fred Fieldgate, 'it shouldn't he here – a *silver-spotted skipper*.' But it was there – number fifty-seven – a hoped for one-butterfly-day had turned into an unexpected two-butterfly-day.

The *silver-spotted skipper* was in long grass – its absent friends like short grass. As we drove on into short grazed rabbit country so the rare *silver-spotted skipper* became the common *silver-spotted skipper*. What a pretty little butterfly – with its distinctive silver spots. Not only were there *skippers* and short grass – but rock rose-covered ant hills – not by the hundred, or thousand, but by the million. Someone with time on his or her hands has counted 3 million ant hills at Porton Down and over 30 billion ants. I hope they are not genetically modified or given exotic viruses – they could take over the world.

Wednesday August 14th

9.00am Where's Nigel? I hope he is not wearing pink socks – but I need to be away to the Lake District to see the *Scotch argus*. The weather forecast says that the morning will be sunny and the afternoon will be cloudy – and according to the books the *Scotch argus* only flies in sunlight. But then some of the same books also say that the *Scotch argus* can only be seen in Scotland – but there are at least two colonies in England – one in the Lake District and the other in the Pennines. I must hope that the weather forecast is wrong – it has been wrong so often this summer perhaps it should be transferred to the BBC's light entertainment department.

10.00am Where's Nigel? Perhaps he's looking for his pink socks and can't find them. The morning was sunny – but already clouds are appearing – perhaps I should fly to the Lake District – but where would I land? This mad, bad Labour Government has just announced more runways and airports: it is hardly believable – carbon dioxide is increasing year by year: Britain's temperature is reckoned to increase by 3 degrees by 2050 and so what is Fatty John Prescott's answer – more aeroplanes. If some of our MPs had brains, they would be dangerous. To make matters worse of course, a huge group of Government Ministers, MPs and officials will soon be going on a gigantic junket to Johannesburg for the Earth Summit – to discuss the drastic environmental action needed to save life on Earth as we know it – ho, ho, ho. Long-term actions by short-term politicians – ho, ho, ho.

This government intends seven new major runways on greenfield sites around London. It is a Third World mentality – grand airports to impress visiting politicians while chaos reigns on roads and rails. Zambia has a most impressive airport – I wonder if the lovely Tony is now basing his transport policies on Zambia?

It is amazing – the government claims to want to reduce global warming emissions – while backing globalisation, the free market and importing food and products that we could produce here – thus really reducing emissions. There are more transport planes being built than passenger planes – lorry sizes are regularly being increased by EU decree and it can only be a matter of time before some intellectual MP announces: 'We must have another Channel Tunnel to ensure the financial future of Britain.' Nobody will have told him or her that we actually import more from Europe than we export.

Amazingly too, with British farming on its knees and new wheat at its lowest price for decades – just £50 per ton – some broiler fowl producers in Yorkshire and East Anglia, so it is said, are importing wheat for their turkeys and hens from Hungary and Poland at £41 per ton. There's vision and sustainable trading for you. Some of the land now being ploughed in Hungary is to grow cheap wheat that will put British farmers out of business – praise be to globalisation and the free market — it is also one of the last strongholds of the Great Bustard — who cares when you can eat cheap turkey burgers? One company selling broiler fowl proclaims that its produce comes from 'the heart of the country'. Which country — Poland or Hungary? That is what we want to know.

11.00am Where's Nigel?

11.05am Nigel has arrived — wearing blue socks — not pink socks — is he well? And why does he think 11.15 is early morning? Eric has a long way to take us before we get anywhere near a *Scotch argus*. I think we will use the A1 as our major north/south gas guzzling runway.

The sun was shining brightly, now it's only shining when it's not behind a cloud. 'Don't worry,' reassured blue socks, 'we'll see a *Scotch argus*.' How does he know? Nigel is too relaxed — he doesn't seem to realise the importance of the *Scotch argus* — NUMBER FIFTY-EIGHT.

12.30pm Newark — the sun is still shining sometimes — the River Trent is still flowing all the time.

1.30pm Ferrybridge — the power station stands next to the road belching out smoke like a temple built to the God of Global Warming. And the temple gives us power — power to run our videos, hair curlers, plunge pool and computer games — the necessities of life — how we love the temple at Ferrybridge and all

the others exactly like it – it gives us warmth, security and power. I hope no butterfly tries to fly over it – the draft of hot air would carry it high up into the upper atmosphere – rather like flying over John Prescott with his mouth open.

As the smoke and steam from Ferrybridge rises up in a great pillar of pollution, it fans out into cloud – permanent cloud. Westwards is more cloud – and where will westwards be soon – the Lake District – home of the sunshine flying *Scotch argus*.

2.30pm We are level with the Lakes now and a large bank of cloud runs east-west. Westwards is thick cloud, eastwards is sun. Westwards is the Lake District; eastwards is I know not where and what is more I do not care.

2.35pm The sun has gone. Blue socks can drive – I can't watch – I'm going to sleep. Am I suffering from paranoia – or acute paranoia?

3.35pm It's drizzling – it's grey – welcome to the Lake District. Does the *Scotch argus* ever wash? It can drizzle-wash today if it wants to.

4.00pm We arrive at Arnside Knott – not just Arnside – but Arnside Knott. It is a place of unexpected beauty overlooking a river estuary flowing into Morecombe Bay. Britain is a place of so many hidden and unexpected beauties – I'm sure the planners and developers will find them all in due course.

Will we find the *Scotch argus*? According to the experts it flies from July, week four, to August, week two, and it is already past August week two; if I have missed it here – then it will have to be a rush to Scotland where the flying time is slightly later.

The drizzle had brought out the smell of oak and pine on the lower slopes of this odd chunk of limestone – and then, we both saw it, a butterfly. It had the flopping flight of a *ringlet* or *meadow brown* – but it was flying – in drizzle – no, no, not the *drizzled skipper* again! It settled on a low bramble flower with its wings open – dark wings with red patches broken by black spots with white centres – it was an English-living, drizzle-flying, bramble-resting, *SCOTCH ARGUS* – number *FIFTY-EIGHT* – mission accomplished – a wonderful, wonderful, beautiful, sad, funny, exciting mission – I felt a sudden surge of happiness – *number fifty-eight* – the beautiful – the glorious, the *Scotch argus* – I could have kissed it – I could have snogged it. Is it legal to kiss a butterfly? Is it legal to kiss any animal? I'm sure the way things are going it will soon be legal to marry animals in London – even compulsory – oh how pretty – Ken Livingstone walking down the aisle with a newt. Anybody pointing out that London has lost the plot, that the distance in understanding between nature and urban Britain can now only be measured in light years will be arrested for provocation; yes, 'Londoners demand the 'right' to marry animals'. I can see it now in banner headlines. I decided not to kiss the butterfly, I looked at Nigel in triumph – his face was a mass of smiles – no I would not kiss him either – pink socks or blue socks – what a pity Sarah didn't make this trip. 'There you are, I told you there was nothing to worry about,' Nigel gloated after his accident, rather than design.

There was not just one *Scotch argus* – they were everywhere. For some reason Arnside Knott suits their every need and they are clearly flourishing. Why they do not flourish in the rest of the Lake District I have no idea – ask a *Scotch argus*.

Higher up the hill were wind-sculpted yews and junipers – hundreds of miles from Porton Down but the same combination.

On top of the hill there was a man with his son – not a butterfly with its caterpillar. There was no wind to sculpt yews or junipers, or to fly a kite – yet he was trying to fly a kite. How can you fly a kite with no wind – you have to be a butterfly – a *Scotch argus* to fly at Arnside Knott with no wind.

He was wearing the uniform of a British middle-class man on holiday – shirt outside his shorts – shorts nearly down to his white, white knees – cotton socks halfway up his white, white shins and Jesus sandals that are only used once a year on holiday. *Homo absurdicus* is usually found on National Trust properties – sometimes in herds – throughout England, and Arnside Knott is a National Trust property. I could not bear the sight of him trying to fly a kite in no wind – so I decided to watch butterflies – the wonderful, the brilliant *Scotch argus* – *number* *FIFTY-EIGHT*.

'Shall we have a drink Nigel? Shall we drink Champagne?'

Two middle-aged men drinking Champagne in the corner of the Talbot bar – thank goodness Nigel couldn't find his pink socks.

Thank you Gordon Beningfield – friend of the countryside, friend of country people, friend of mine and above all friend and painter of butterflies – thank you for giving me such a good year.

Thursday August 15th

Still in the Lake District – will I be lucky and see another butterfly – number fifty-nine? There is certainly a remote chance of seeing a *monarch*, being so close to the west coast but virtually no chance of seeing a *Camberwell beauty*.

Beauty is in the eye of the beholder – well, according to the local paper, the *Westmorland Gazette*, the gorgeous, pouting, Liverpool lovely, Cherie Blair, was on holiday here recently, along with two of her children and her wonderfully gifted husband. They spent all of three days in the Lakes before flying off to somewhere warmer and foreign. The newspapers had their photo opportunities, the Blairs were here – the Discount Duo were seen supporting Britain's tourist industry – briefly.

It is odd, Bomber Blair having a holiday in an area of Britain where his own policies lead to devastation and to the illegal slaughter of millions of sheep and cattle. Yet nobody arrested him and of course nobody will. Sadly in Britain today we no longer see the rule of law, just the political manipulation of the law.

According to reports, the Blair entourage did not visit a farm – but it did visit 'Peter Rabbit and Friends' and rode on a toy railway. I'm sure that made all the farmers going broke and the traditional Lake District foot hunters, threatened with the loss of their hounds, feel a lot better. If only the Blairs had stayed on to visit the Vale of Rydal Sheep Dog Trials and Hound Show with me – they might have learnt something and met some real people.

Last year's show should have been the Centenary – but was cancelled because of foot and mouth – as a result this year's show was packed – a mixture of

foxhounds, beagles, harriers, terriers, sheep dog trialing, hound-trailing and stick-making; it must be one of the most traditional shows in the country – a celebration of the local culture of the Lakes – so while in the area for butterflies, I felt I had to support a community under siege. I spoke to old friends and made new ones. I met two women who – even a year after foot and mouth cried on my shoulder at the loss of their animals. I ate and drank with people who were trying to laugh again – trying to forget – trying to forget. But how can they forget as they are now faced with a new threat from our ignorant, urban government – the threat to ban – to kill – their hounds – more tears – more crying – more dying – they do not want it or seek it.

Here the hounds don't stay in their kennels, in their packs, during the summer when they are not hunting – they go out to the farms – hundreds of country families – farmers and shepherds, look after hounds, and hounds are beautiful, remarkable animals.

Here were people who love dogs – sheep dogs and hunting dogs, whose fathers and grandfathers before them – and Beatrix Potter – stopped work to follow the famous Fell packs – the Blencathra, the Coniston, the Ullswater, the Lunsdale, the Melbreak and the Eskdale and Ennerdale. Here was an emotional cocktail of history, hope, culture and fear. Here were their dogs Ranter, Talisman, Woodman, Ranger, Rainbow, Dalesman and Bellman. Several times as I saw men and dogs, girlfriends and puppies doing what they have always done – a lump came to my throat.

No – there was no sign of Mr and Mrs Blair at the Rydal Show. They prefer other cultures for their main holidays – with just a glimpse of Peter Rabbit and photographers before making for the airport – **Camberwell beauties** or **Downing Street emperors**? I don't think so – just the human forms of **dingy skipper**.

Thursday August 22nd

After all the rushing from one end of the country to the other I have actually been in the same place for a whole week – at home – on the farm – what a pleasure and today St Swithin actually got it right. The sun shone all day. We have been getting the straw bales in – for the cattle's 'winter bedding'. It is barley straw, so they can eat it too – eating your bedding – the height of relaxation and luxury – breakfast in bed.

We finished in mid-afternoon – the Dutch barn is nearly full and the straw is dry – the cattle will be comfortable for the whole winter.

Butterfly success, and now my harvest home – I felt euphoric – so we had something alcoholic – good Herefordshire cider – apples turned into sparkling, liquid happiness.

Friday August 23rd

I'm off again. I feel guilty. Yes, I did see a **grayling** – one solitary **grayling** – for all of one second, on the way to see the **silver-studded blues**. Perhaps I should see it for slightly longer and not from inside a car, looking out.

Holme dunes – yes, the North Norfolk coast again and not a nudist in sight. There were many fully clothed – well, holiday-clothed loungers, in sight and a couple taking a dog lead for a walk. How strange – two strollers – one dog lead and no dog in a nature reserve. Then I saw it and jammed on Eric's brakes, to skid-stop in my own miniature sand storm – a light coloured retriever-type dog was in full pursuit of the Norfolk Wildlife Trust's sheep. They were 'conservation sheep' – used by the Trust to graze the dunes, and kept in by an electric fence. It was a baking hot day and the dog had managed to divide the little flock into two; one group was stationary – looking apprehensive, and panting. The other was being chased – while the dog lead walkers strolled along in complete oblivion or delirium.

I jumped out of the car and hurdled the fence – fortunately it had been knocked down already. The gist of what I said was, 'I say lovely little dog would you mind not chasing the sheep old boy and excuse me lovely holidaymakers – I hope it is not too inconvenient for you to retrieve your delightful companion animal and re-attach it to your lead?' Why do people always believe that their pet dog will never kill sheep – four years ago I had several of my beautiful beasts killed by an unknown dog.

Both dog and man seemed to understand my tone and use of English and beat a hasty retreat. How could a man with half a brain – and a wife the colour of a sun-baked cow pat walk through a nature reserve while their dog undertook a piece of seaside sheep-worrying? If only it was *unbelievable*, but now when town visits country it is all too *believable*.

I alerted the warden who tore off in pursuit of the two grockles and their dog, creating a sand storm of his own. '**Grayling**' he said as he departed, 'they're still about – 'try the Buddleia by the Visitors' Centre.'

Visitors' Centre? Buddleia? Not a **grayling** in sight. The dunes were not so high as those at Holkham – less cover for butterflies, bathing beauties and

giggling gays – there's a flopping brown butterfly – a **meadow brown** – and another – it
landed on my foot – it landed on my
defumigated trainers – now after a summer of wear – well and truly fumigated
again. It is very difficult looking round
your stomach and down onto a butterfly to
identify it when it's settled on your foot
with its wings closed. Several others followed suit – but not at the same time. I
wonder what the collective noun for a
group of foot-resting butterflies would be – a
boot of butterflies – a knot – or even a verruca?

'How do you tell a **grayling** from any other
flopping butterfly?' I asked the Warden on his
returns. 'They often settle on your feet,' he
replied. Not one of my six butterfly
books contained this piece of simple
information – it would have made life
much simpler if they had.

SEPTEMBER

Sunday September 1st

A new month, a mellow month, a fruiting month. I walked up the railway line again – my butterfly walk – but where have all the butterflies gone – where are the wings, where is the flutter? One month, one week, one day they are there and then suddenly they have gone – vanished – there are still flowers – tatty, fading flowers – there is still fruit – ripening fruit – but suddenly the butterflies have gone- not all of them – not quite – there goes a **meadow brown** – on its last wings – tattered and torn and a **cabbage white** – even worse – how do they fly and when do they die – suddenly – soon – the wings of spring and summer fade away.

How lucky I have been – the deserted railway line shows that once the time for a butterfly to flutterby has come, it quickly goes. I just saw the **marsh fritillary** – almost the last of the year's **marsh fritillaries**, the **northern brown argus**, the **small mountain ringlet** and the **Scotch argus** – seen by a whisker, or a wingbeat. Will my luck hold to see a **monarch** or a **Camberwell beauty**?

Monday September 2nd

Oh no; I need a million pounds, and quick. The sale of Turnastone Court Farm has fallen through and it has been offered to the Countryside Restoration Trust after all. I will have to find my begging bowl.

More good news – I'm publishing a book *The Feather and the Furrow* of stunning wildlife photographs – minus butterflies – by my Vice Chairman of the CRT – Chris Knights – farmer, conservationist and wildlife photographer. His broad Norfolk accent suggests peasant; his farming and photography suggest a shrewd businessman. The good – astonishing – news is that I have managed to sell 2,500 copies of his book to Tesco – as Chris grows millions of carrots and parsnips for Tesco. He was so excited when he heard the news – while driving to Scotland to take more photographs – that he filled his Range Rover with £54-worth of petrol: it's a pity it only runs on diesel.

To the pub for dinner/lunch to celebrate Turnastone and Tesco – oh dear – did I really write that? I will have to burn the pen. If only butterflies played football – they would be so popular: talk over steak and kidney pie was not of fifty-eight species of butterfly – but of David Beckham and his wife – pop singer – a 'Spice Girl' – 'Posh Spice' – although she doesn't sound posh.

Pubs can be nasty intemperate places. I believed nothing that I heard. My rather brutal companions claimed that after Mr Beckham had played football for Manchester United, the couple travelled to London to fit the birth of their child into their busy celebrity schedule. Then, Mrs Beckham had a baby by caesarean section – to save time and pain – she was 'too posh to push'. How can they say such outrageous, wrong, unbelievable things? Butterflies have no such problems – they don't play football.

Alas the bar-stool nastiness does not stop there – the baby is being named Romeo – it's not his fault. Nothing wrong with Romeo – their first child is named Brooklyn – that is where Mrs Beckham discovered she was pregnant – lucky it wasn't Pidly-cum-Fenton, Ugly or the Orkney village of Twatt. If butterflies did the same thing there would be thousands of butterflies called *Bramble Patch*, *Meadow*, and *Hedgerow*.

Romeo is a perfectly good name. There must be thousands of little Romeos throughout Britain. But perhaps they meant to name it Rome and got the spelling wrong – or was it meant to be Roma the football team – who knows – ask the Beckhams. If it really was a fashionable/convenience birth – how will they arrange a fashionable/convenience death – one to save time and pain – I wonder? Perhaps it will be euthanasia by sound – play the Spice Girls' music just one more time.

I prefer the story of Christine and Barry to 'Posh and Becks'. Christine and Barry are CRT volunteers and they love butterflies – they are CRT butterfly counters. They bought a boat and Christine felt unwell. It's not nice, feeling unwell at the age of 46. Twenty-eight weeks later she went to the doctor: 'You're pregnant' he told her, 'you have been for twenty-eight weeks.' Oh dear, twenty years after the birth of her twins she's having another baby. Christine gave birth by caesarean section to save her life. *Hello* magazine did not want pictures of the baby. After buying the boat and with the example of Posh and Becks in view, 'What will the baby be called?' everybody asked – 'Marina?' She was called Eleanor. She will not have a celebrity lifestyle but she will be taught the beauty of butterflies.

Tuesday September 3rd

What a terrible way to start the day – I nearly choked on my cornflakes. There, staring out of the paper at me, Prime Minister Tony Blair and Zimbabwe's President, Robert Mugabe. I don't think they like each other, I don't like either of them and Mr Mugabe has been very rude about Mr Blair.

I regard Blair as Britain's Mugabe – put them both in a sack – it wouldn't matter which one came out first. In Zimbabwe, Mugabe is driving white farmers off the land. In Britain, Blair is getting rid of even more, through his policies, and from the 64 farming suicides a year, as far as I am concerned, Bomber has blood on his hands. Oh – and it seems that Blair now wants to get involved with another war – with Iraq again – he is a very macho man with countries that can't hit back – he is the original Viagra Drip. Who knows one day he may even declare war on butterflies.

Mugabe hates Blair – he also hates homosexuals and of course at one time it seemed as if Bomber had bought a job lot from Fairy Land to half fill his cabinet. But Comrade Mugabe has had a great mental lapse. He seems to have forgotten that Zimbabwe's first President after black rule – President Canaan Banana, turned out to be a bent Banana, and quickly disappeared from view.

I dare not read Blair's speech from the Earth Summit. I suppose he was on about saving Africa again, from whichever luxury hotel he happened to be staying in at the time. There will have been a bit about reducing the use of fossil fuels to prevent global warming – then the triumphant ending – more globalisation – to increase the use of fossil fuels and accelerate global warming. Good brain Mr Blair – he went to public school and Oxford you know – please take note Mr Booker.

The best quote I have ever heard about Africa suits Blair right down to the ground. 'After three weeks in Africa you want to write a book. After three months you want to write an article. After three years you realise how little you know, and you want to write nothing at all.' Mr Anon is a very perceptive man. Mugabe's trouble is that he is really a sun-baked Yorkshireman – Mugabe spelt backwards reads e-ba-gum.

Wednesday September 4th

Good heavens – I might be wrong about Tony Blair after all. He could be far shrewder than I thought. The great conclusion of the Earth Summit is more sanitation for Africa – which in everyday language means – more lavatories for

Africa. So – after transporting world leaders, cabinet ministers, advisors and bureaucrats by the thousand to Johannesburg – the big conclusion is not more butterflies – but more lavatories for Africa – a rush to flush. More water flowing down the drain in a continent already short of water – well that's good news – but here's the clever bit. More lavatories in Zimbabwe could mean more oestrogen (the female pill) in the water – which could create more Canaan Bananas in Zimbabwe. If he drinks enough, it could even turn President Mugabe gay – what a triumph for Tony Blair.

Tony Blair, our great Prime Minister, world leader, may be even craftier still. Already in Zimbabwe there is a primitive toilet called 'The Blair'; yes, invented years ago by a Mr Blair, and so in the world of long-drops and short-drops the name of Blair could become as immortalised as that of the great Dr Crapper – an earlier pioneer of the lavatorial world. This means that wherever the Blair's toilet reigns supreme – people talking rubbish could soon be accused of talking Blair – the sheep of the Lake District would readily agree. It also means that whenever anybody has to rush off to the toilet – the first word that would enter their head is 'Blair'.

The hard-pressed Zimbabweans would love all this as they have a great sense of humour – based on laughing at themselves. The latest joke is – Why do Zimbabweans have the greatest I.Q. in the world? I.Q. for petrol. I.Q. for bread. I.Q. for mealie meal etc. I wonder if President Mugabe or President Blair laugh at themselves?

Sunday September 8th

Westwards again towards wind-blown **monarchs**. After a chilly starlit night I arrived at Frampton Country Fair in Gloucestershire. They want me to rouse up the natives to get them to go on the Countryside March on September 22nd. With another rousing tomorrow in Pembrokeshire – I will be moving deep into potential **monarch** territory.

The Countryside March is not quite what it says. It is not a march through the countryside – but a march through London to tell members of our delightful urban government that farming is

dying, rural communities are falling apart, our country culture is being crushed and that the matter of people chasing furry little hen-eating animals ought to be a matter of individual conscience, not government edict.

Isn't it odd? Britain is supposed to be a multicultural society – but our own rural culture is forever under attack – quite often by the politically correct – the very people who sing the praises of other minority cultures.

Because of this, I started my little rousing by saying: 'In case any of you are of a fragile disposition and easily offended please go for a walk round the lake and come back when I have finished. If there is a black, vegetarian, Muslim, asylum-seeking, one-legged, lesbian lorry driver present then you may be offended at what I am going to say, as I want the same rights that you have got already.' It got a laugh – and afterwards people seemed keen to get marching.

Monday September 9th

Abergavenny – yes, back to Wayills, boyo – to spend a million pounds that I haven't got. A deal was done and the CRT will get Turnastone Court Farm in Herefordshire – now all we need is a large loan and a lot of faith, hope and charity.

It is a long winding road to Pembrokeshire, made even longer by the drizzle. Do *monarch* butterflies fly in drizzle? If they are halfway across the Atlantic with two more days of flying to go, they have no other option. The Atlantic looked cold and grey with American air coming in fast as a westerly wind. Sadly, it carried no American butterflies – drive on, Blue Socks!

It was extraordinary. At Castle Martin there is a firing range – a firing range for tanks and tanks were firing – firing over a chunk of wild attractive country-side – what? It looks as if Tony Blair has declared war on butterflies – shells, explosions and bursts of automatic fire – I hope no outgoing shells were hitting incoming *monarchs*.

It is very strange – there is a public viewing area as part of the tank firing range and there were two people viewing – with a *D* for *Deutchsland* on their car. German tourists on the very west of Britain watching tanks firing – the Pembrokeshire Panzers. It is good to see that the German war genes are still flourishing after all these years. The two tank watchers were built like tanks. They were not just fat or built for comfort, they were huge. They were not 'Desert Rats', but German Fats. Where most people have mounds they had mountains – bulging under lycra body-hugging shorts and shirts – as if they had been force-fed blancmange. It was not a pretty sight – heaving rolls of blubber – straining to get out. From the general areas of bulge, I took it that one was male and the other was female. How two such specimens would mate defies both description and imagination. How either of them could climb through the turret of a tank would pose anther problem. Nigel wanted to take a photograph but he had forgotten his wide-angle lens.

We found the Old Rectory – now without a rector – but with a pleasant couple leading the good life, doing bed and breakfast and organising coaches from Pembrokeshire for the Countryside March. She had an interesting past – she was once courted by a fine upstanding Army officer; unbeknown to her he was really a bad down-lying cad – a bounder – as he was also taking his hat off to a Princess – hence the relationship became somewhat crowded.

Suddenly there was screaming – was someone horse-whipping the bounder, or had a butterfly been hit by a shell? It stopped; it started again – and we all rushed towards the source of the sound – a small-walled garden. Astonishingly, there was one of the Germans on all fours – head in the mud, screaming – wait a minute, it's not a German – it's a pot-bellied pig. The poor, unfortunate pot-belly had been rootling in the garden and had somehow managed to get a piece of old buried wire trapped around a tooth. The beast was held hard and every time it tried to move – it squealed and protested. I managed a quick snip with wire-cutters and pot-belly was free. It was remarkable; I swear that the pig smiled at me – I had become the hero of a pot-bellied pig.

That was not the only remarkable thing about the Old Rectory – from the front windows – the view was rustic – pure countryside. From the back windows the view was pure global warming – there was a green valley and then showing above the next, a tangle of pipes, chimneys and flames of the Milford Haven Oil Refinery. Sometimes when the wind is wrong, a fine drizzle of oil settles on the Old Rectory – but never mind it's quite harmless, the experts say so. In any case, I have been reassured about oil – on the drive across Wales I picked up a leaflet – 'Climate Change – Our View' published by Esso. Silly me – I didn't realise how wrong I have been all these years and that the world's large oil companies are really the harbingers of good. With the oil companies being environmentally aware the world is safe. I do apologise.

The meeting in Pembroke Town Hall went well – the message was: march, join the CRT and save our butterflies. Afterwards at supper I met a man who wanted to do all three and he became a Life Member of the CRT on the spot. He was also one of the few people I have ever met who welcomes global warming – he owns a nudist camp.

Tuesday September 10th

Driving all day again. Nigel's got his pink socks on again. We stop somewhere that looks vaguely familiar – it's home – I live here.

Eric – the postman, has left a letter. Someone has been complaining about my speech at Frampton-on-Severn to the local Gloucestershire paper. They have even complained to the Chief Constable of Gloucestershire – a Dr Brain – the *politically correct* are complaining – *informing* – about the *politically incorrect*. Funny that, I thought Britain was supposed to be the country founded on free speech, freedom and democracy. How times change. It can only be a matter of time before George Orwell's 'thought police' arrive on my doorstep – courtesy of a European Directive – or a New Labour purge. Apparently Dr Brain is well into political crime, as is a lady Commander in London, Commander Dick. I wonder what name Dick and Brain would choose if they got married?

Thursday September 12th

Thursday – it must be the Lakes again. Ah, Yes – the Westmorland County Agricultural Show. In return for yet another Countryside March rousing for the locals – the CRT has been given a table in a tent to display its wares.

If only I could display my entry badge – I've lost it – and they won't let me in; give people a badge or uniform and it's like the Third Reich all over again. So after leaving at 4 o'clock in the morning – travelling 250 miles – charging no fee – a man with a badge will not let us in. Nigel is so furious that his blood pressure has risen and his blue socks have turned pink.

When this modern member of the Waffen SS was looking elsewhere – we drove in behind him – good old Eric.

What a lovely show; a real farming country show. The first big farming show in the Lakes since foot and mouth. To ensure that no new infection starts, visitors from the sheep have to walk over a disinfected mat and wipe their hands with a 'wipe' – very effective – especially as the foot and mouth virus's favourite cubby hole is the nose. Anything less than a disinfectant stirrup-pump full up each nostril would be waste of time – it was a waste of time.

The NFU – called the National Farmers Union by some and the 'No ...... Use' by others – was considered by many to be a waste of time during foot and mouth. So while Nigel manned the CRT table I sought out the NFU stand to see how it was fighting for farming.

At the NFU members' lunch tent – nothing. 'Go to our stand in the organisations marquee.' The stand was deserted – the only pamphlet was a series of cartoons about cows – 'It's a Cow's Life – Millie's Story and Udder Stuff.' Very impressive – I now know which version of NFU I consider to be the most appropriate.

Good heavens, a whole stand devoted not to butterflies – but to one of my favourite fruits – damsons – how I love them. Apparently damsons do very well in the Lake District.

My eye caught a pile of pamphlets – I don't believe it – is this the Lakes or Zimbabwe – what – '*Bent Banana Disease*'? Is this the autobiography of Canaan Banana – or real life? Fortunately it was real life, as Bent Banana Disease is a real disease of damsons: when it strikes the fruit shrinks and looks like little bent bananas.

I bought a bottle of damson wine to finish off a good day. Years ago I bought a bottle of Kenyan wine – it was disgusting – like drinking alcoholic Windowlene – this batch of damson wine came from the same school of wine appreciation.

Monday September 16th

I have got a problem at the moment. When I get up in the morning and look into the mirror, I don't recognise myself. The face that looks back at me is thin and rugged; if I had blue eyes instead of brown it would look vaguely like Clint Eastwood in his prime. I have to confess that my eyes are not particularly good first thing in the morning.

In bed I have more trouble; if I try to roll over I am stopped by something hard. For the first time since last year's bale-carting, I can feel my stomach muscles: if I lie on my front it is like lying on a sheet of corrugated iron – unless the springs in my mattress have gone. Perhaps I had better take another look. But what is for certain is that I am getting fit. I am certainly fitter than Colin the cucumber: he struggles on – I have never seen a cucumber plant so desperately in need of an overall stem and leaf massage. Perhaps even more is needed – how do you give a cucumber plant called Colin the kiss of life? Perhaps a sap-transfusion would help.

Despite the hours sitting in and on Eric, rushing from one side of the country to the other, I am losing weight. The reason is simple – I need to be fit for the Countryside March next Sunday, and then the day after we fly off to the Dark Continent for another attempt to climb Kilimanjaro. But will I get to the top again – eleven years and one and a half stone later? There is another matter too: a Kenyan friend, Joe, has climbed the mountain twice, with a twenty year gap between climbs. He was shocked at the retreat of Kilimanjaro's glaciers and it convinced him that global warming was far more serious than the politicians suppose. Perhaps he should read Esso's little pamphlet for some reassurance. I wonder if I will have a similar jolt?

I will be in a group rounded up by the CRT. My ascent will, of course, be drug-assisted – anti-wheeze inhalers, plus soluble aspirin to keep my blood as thin as the air. I have also been told to take Diamox, a drug for pre-menstrual tension. Apparently it helps to counteract altitude sickness in men, as opposed to attitude sickness in women. I hope I am not expected to wear high heels and suspenders as well.

Now for the confession; as a lifelong asthmatic my fitness-level can get very low, particularly in winter, when often I feel barely alive. At the moment however, it is quite high, as all of this year's small straw and hay bales have been safely manhandled into the barn. But in addition, I have been advised by a health freak friend to 'power walk' every day; 'walk briskly for twenty minutes a day, followed by twenty press-ups and the fat will melt away!' The trouble is that I never walk 'briskly' around the farm; if I see birds, butterflies, hares, foxes or muntjac deer, I want to watch them – consequently I stroll, and 'power walk' does not feature in my vocabulary.

As a result, oh dear, what a confession – it sounds dreadful; I have purchased a running machine – or in my case a waddling machine – to get fit for the March and Kilimanjaro. What an investment. It means that I power-waddle in my living room while watching football on the television or listening to Madonna. I can even read while I'm waddling, which can be very dangerous, particularly if you laugh so much that you stop walking – you can be shot off backwards onto the sideboard.

Of course having to get a waddling machine is another indication of just how discriminated against country people can be. Londoners get giant running machines provided absolutely free, only there they are called 'escalators'. Why so many Londoners join 'gyms' I have no idea when all they have to do is walk *up* the *down* escalator.

Sunday September 22nd

The day of the Countryside March for *Liberty and Livelihood* has dawned, but already it has almost turned into a marathon. No trains were running from Cambridge station so I had to drive to Stevenage to catch a train that was actually working. Stevenage – oh dear – if only John Betjeman had been to Stevenage before Slough – sadly 'Come lovely bombs and fall on Stevenage' does not have quite the same ring to it.

Stevenage was once a quiet country town – now it is a London overspill depository – working-class as opposed to the more affluent criminal-class over-spills of Essex. It means that the male necklaces and bangles of Stevenage are fake gold instead of the real thing.

A perfect fake cockney caricature was on the platform once we had bought the tickets 'Cor blimey mate – it's about time you *bumpkins* got what you deserve.'

Bumpkins? I wonder what he calls Asians, West Indians or one-legged lesbian lorry drivers? I tried to phone Sarah on my mobile phone once the train had arrived – but I had problems. Fortunately an eight-year-old boy was on hand to sort out the technical difficulties.

The train was full of tweeds, tatty Barbours, badges, banners, and according to 'Cor blimey mate' – bumpkins. The intention was to 'hangout' with Sarah – 'cool, wicked' – but how do you find an eight-stone, muesli-eating, Butterfly Safariist among thousands – hundreds of thousands, of large beef-eating sons of the soil and assorted maidens of the meadows? Sarah was of course representing the Hammersmith countryside.

There were ruddy faces, rrrrolling accents, angry banners, and marching wellies – all obscuring Sarah. I told her I would meet her under a tree in Hyde Park. There are hundreds of trees in Hyde Park – all were surrounded by a huge mass of moving people.

Sarah was lost in the sea of humanity. However, I bumped into a gaggle of yet more Londoners – marching for the countryside – who I hadn't seen for years. They were bad people – they appeared not to like our great leader Mr Blair. Without any warning, for those with a delicate disposition, one of them asked: 'What is the difference between Mr Blair and a sperm? A sperm has a 200 million-to-one chance of becoming human.' In my view that was most unfair – on the sperm.

The banners showed an almost frightening hatred of the nice Mr Blair – hardly surprising with 288 farmers and workers leaving the land every week and one farming suicide every six days. One banner gave an interesting insight into the morality of New Labour: 'Bombing Iraq ✓; Buggering Boys ✓; Smoking

Dope ✓: Chasing Foxes ✗'. Another proclaimed 'Blair, Britain's Mugabe'. In Britain, President Blair is getting rid of even more farmers through his policies than Comrade Mugabe – yet nobody says a word.

The marchers were marching for all sorts of activities and issues – farming, villages, village halls, rural post offices, hunting, shooting, fishing, more rural policemen, schools, pubs, Uncle Tom Cobbley and all. I was marching for all of these things plus *butterflies*. As farming becomes more intense *butterfly* numbers fall, as more chemical sprays are used *butterfly* numbers fall; as development increases, *butterfly* numbers fall; as politicians produce hot air – talking conservation instead of doing conservation – *butterfly* numbers fall; so I was marching for *butterflies*. We shuffled, shouted, whistled, smiled and laughed our way through London – crossing the counting line at 300,000 – what a cheer went up.

It had been thirsty work; barmen and barmaids were being rushed off their feet. It is the first time I have been in a pub when it was drunk dry; incredibly it was shortly followed by a second.

Of course not only were there people marching *for* things; there were also people marching *against* things – Blair, the delightful Mrs Blair, the BBC, Brussels, the CAP, supermarkets and politicians all summed up by the banner 'Bring Back Guy Fawkes'. Oh dear there was even one proclaiming 'Robin Page for Prime Minister' – I don't think so somehow.

At 400,000 an even bigger cheer went up. That was when I bumped into Kilimanjaro-climbing Christopher Booker who was definitely marching against Brussels and the CAP. It was possibly the biggest demonstration in British history – a demonstration for the countryside and for butterflies amounting to 407,791 indignant individuals.

But the big question is, did that figure include Sarah? At 5' 1$\frac{3}{4}$" was she seen and was she counted? She is demanding a recount.

Monday September 23rd

Will I have to get my shiny black leather shoes out again – my funeral shoes? Colin the cucumber is looking far from well. I watered him and pulled up some bellvine that was in danger of strangling him – a cucumber life hangs in the balance.

Tuesday September 24th

I woke up late. The sun was streaming through the window and there were butterflies, white ones and yellow ones dancing over the grass. There were birds too – not singing or perching – they were standing on long thick legs – they were ostriches; it's Tuesday, it must be Africa. And there in front of the Land Rover – near, clear and very high, complete with glaciers, was Mount Kilimanjaro. Oh dear, it seems that over the next few days I am going to suffer again. It will be my third climb of this beautiful, dreadful mountain – I will be climbing and suffering when I should be at home waiting for news of wandering **monarchs** and **Camberwell beauties** – and giving Colin intensive care.

This trip is all Christopher Booker's fault. Partly due to our mutual friendship with the late, and much missed Sir Laurens van der Post, we have been promising ourselves an African adventure for years – including the ascent of the mighty Mount Kilimanjaro. This year I put my foot down: 'Booker, do it,' I ordered – that is how you have to speak to ageing ex-public schoolboys – 'or at your stage of tobacco intake, with your pension book about to fall though your letter box, you will be on a stairlift before you know it and incapable of climbing anything.'

So here we are, with thirteen others from the CRT in the middle of the heat and dust of Amboseli about to climb that mountain. We are a motley crew – scientists, engineers, Booker's two sons and one pneumatically chested girlfriend –

destined never to drown – my bald GP cousin Duncan, Alan and Tilly without their reindeer, a hill runner, Vivienne a literary agent, a Yank, and an alco-pops sipping clubette – no – wait – beneath the shade of a thorn tree I see a pink butterfly hairgrip and a pink butterfly T-shirt – it's Sarah fluttering by again. Oh, and there was one more – Howie, an Aussie – an Aussie who loves butterflies; what next? An Australian who reads poetry – no – that is going just a bit too far.

As we ate a picnic lunch washed down with Tusker and Diet-Coke, under the solitary thorn – some of the group were already *Blixenating*. The verb '*to Blixenate*' is taken from Karen Blixen – the *Out of Africa* dreamer, whose dreams and loves ended in tragedy, as well as a beautiful book.

'Robin, it's tremendous – I've had my money's worth already,' said Pete the PhD – *Blixenating* more than most. I clearly should have charged him double. Booker had stopped talking – yes – he was in the early stages; a slow, simmering *Blixenator* usually becomes the most spectacular.

All we had seen so far were elephants, wildebeest, zebra, ostriches, impala and that mountain. I don't think the others had noticed the butterflies – except butterfly-eyed Howie. Our Kenyan leader, Anthony Cheffings – 'Cheffers' –

pointed to a bird. 'That's a fiscal shrike,' he informed us. 'What's fiscal mean?' asked Sarah, using her degree in business studies to the full. Oh dear, what did Tony Blair say was at the heart of his policies: 'Education, edukation, edukashun'. I assume that the fiscal shrike is so called as it looks slightly round shouldered, arrogant and pedantic – like an avian tax inspector.

At Amboseli, on this afternoon, the sights and sounds of ancient Africa were still very close to the surface on these hot, dusty plains. The smell of old Africa is distinctive; a blend of baked sand, flowering thorn and drying grass, mixed with the scent of herbs crushed by the grazers and browsers, and the bleeding, torn limbs of the trees where elephants have walked and fed. Then there are the smells of the animals themselves as they eat, sleep, fight, run, breed and die. Consequently the air you breathe has a dry, pungent, spicy tang – unmistakably the air of Africa – a mixture like no other.

At Amboseli too, on this afternoon, the sights and sounds of new Africa could be seen closing in – advancing, encroaching, changing, crowding, polluting: fire – as a forest burnt on the lower slopes of Kilimanjaro beyond; shining tin – the shanty-town roof tops as more of the world's poor looked for shelter; a jet plane high above – bringing, taking, giving, stealing – produce, people, culture and independence. Africa – what a cocktail – what a problem.

Dr Pete the PhD was glowing pink from the heat and dust. Incredibly Vivienne and Sarah were brown already – as brown as a **monarch**'s wing but not as natural – fake tan comes from plastic bottles. In geology, rocks expand and contract through the heat and cold. Gradually the top layer of the rock lifts, cracks and peels like an onion skin. The process is called exfoliation. These days modern Western women exfoliate too. Fake tan lasts longer on exfoliated skin – how they exfoliate I would not ask and they would not tell – brush, pummy stone, sandpaper, Black and Decker – who cares?

In London's froth and tinsel there are places now for instant tanning: one is even called 'Fake Bake'. Some work rather like a car wash in reverse – for people – squirting out tanning lotion instead of suds and water. With arms and legs apart the spray begins – there is even one girlie wash that employs exciting 'new technology': it claims to use the body's own magnetic field to ensure that no part gets sprayed twice – how exciting. I wonder if the same technology is used for dented cars. With the record of women drivers – both car and driver could then use the same spray simultaneously. It makes the Masai people of the Amboseli Plains seem quite sophisticated.

Wednesday September 25th

Up at dawn to the question: 'Will we see a kill?' Oh what a surprise. *Out of England*, on safari, everybody asks that question, except me. We nearly saw a kill; lions on a warm, dead wildebeest – a few minutes earlier it would have been a warm, live wildebeest. Then we saw a fight as hyenas drove the lions off to steal their breakfast. Dust, claws, blood, tearing flesh and the chilling sounds of a hyena-eating frenzy – welcome to nature, no not the BBC's 'Animal Hospital' with Rolf Harris – welcome to the natural world, minus Rolf Harris – I think I prefer butterflies.

We left Amboseli – three vehicles and three clouds of dust – with memories and photographs locked away. Kilimanjaro kills people, not wildebeest – it kills more people each year than any other mountain in the world through a mixture of altitude sickness, bravado and folly – I took my first Diamox.

Thursday September 26th

'I'm not taking Diamox', informed Dr Duncan, 'I'm going up drug-free.' I took my second Diamox.

At a hut on the edge of the forest we met our porters and guides – all forty of them. In overall charge was a Kikuyu – Joseph – married appropriately to Mary; if only they had a donkey to help me get to the top. Their assistant was the first African I have ever met with a speech impediment – he had a most sp sp sp spec-tacular st st st st stutttttter. It was fortunate that he was from the Pare tribe and not the KKKKKK i kkk u yyyyy u, or his speech of welcome would have lasted all day.

Burning commercial forest – burning to allow re-planting, gave way to natu-ral forest as we walked towards our first campsite. Suddenly I saw the biggest butterfly I have ever seen. It made Sarah's hairgrip seem a very stunted specimen. What was it? Where's Howie? He was reading poetry.

Friday September 27th

The route we are taking is the Loitokitok Trail – which starts just over the Kenyan border in Tanzania. What I did not dare tell the rest of the party was how the route is described in the *Lonely Planet Guide*. It says 'Coming in from the north, this trail is officially closed to the public and, in any case, you're strongly advised to avoid it. Doing the rounds in Nairobi are stories of murders along this route.'

The reason for the murder route is simple: if there is no cloud for the whole ascent then foot by painful foot – stride by agonising stride – the summit can be seen ahead for the full duration of the climb, and there is no cloud. The challenge is in front of us, ever-present: it focuses the mind and subconsciously reduces the pain.

Saturday September 28th

Not only is the summit in focus – but butterflies are too – not plodding up, but flying up Kilimanjaro. What's that? Where's Howie? What a butterfly – it was like a **red admiral** – well almost – but smaller and without the distinctive white spots. It must have been named by an Englishman – it was a **commodore** – not quite of the rank and quality of an **admiral**. It could only have been an Englishman who introduced rank and class into butterfly-land. What next I wonder? The *Debrett's Butterfly Book*, and would Howie read that too? Somewhere, somehow there must be a dingy down-trodden little butterfly called an **able seaman**, eking out an existence where life can hardly survive. Birds have pecking orders: butterflies must have fluttering orders and the **able seaman** would be well below the **commodore** and the **admiral**. But who would be at the top – the **monarch** or the **purple emperor**?

Higher and higher, plod after plod, we must be at thirteen or fourteen thousand feet. For every foot we have climbed Booker has spoken at least three words condemning the EU or Blair's foot and mouth policy, which if recorded would have produced a best-selling book. For a wheezing smoker – who has been receiving Bomber Blair's heating allowance for several years, it is quite an achievement. With a drop in temperature as we climb we will all need the heating allowance before we get to the summit.

'Stop talking Booker. What's that? Where's Howie?' Howie was nowhere to be found – there was the *tiniest* butterfly I have ever seen: the *highest* butterfly I have ever seen. It was a **blue** – a **blue** that made the **small blue** seem large – incredible, but not indelible – I know I will not remember all its finer points when I find *Debrett's Butterfly Book* – I suppose it will be a **peasant blue**, a **midget** or an **oarsman**. Heath and heather gave way to semi-desert and desert – high altitude desert. We all reached Kibo Hut – the final campsite and with only the height of Snowdon to go in the early hours of the morning. Nick, Christopher Booker's eldest son, looked rough. Dr Duncan looked rougher still: 'Can I have a Diamox?' he asked. It was too late – altitude had struck and they were both sent downhill.

171

A cold, high-altitude card school had started. 'What shall we play,' asked Sarah, 'shithead?' Oh no, not that again, I groaned and moaned inwardly, silently, in any case there is nobody who works for the BBC in our party. Sue and Terry were wanting to play cards – they are the nice respectable, middle-class members of the party – Sarah where has your brain gone? 'That's fine,' answered Sue, 'we like shithead, don't we Terry?' So I played high altitude shithead too – I was the one left with all the cards at the end – I was the high altitude shithead – thank you Sarah – thank you Sue and Terry.

Sunday September 29th

'No laughter, no politics – save your breath' ordered Joseph, at one o'clock in the morning. Oh dear it was tough: PhD Pete and the hillrunner gave up; the moon came up as we shuffled higher and higher under Africa's incredible star-filled sky. 'This is really toning up my leg muscles' informed Sarah as she started running on the spot, 'they'll look good in the gym.' How could she be thinking of looking good in the gym when Booker, Cheffers and me were barely alive? What would she do next with her legs – a quick shave or waxing – then a half-atmosphere visit to the Kili Fake-Bake for a quick tan and nail varnish. But at the end of all that, Kilimanjaro would still be 19,342 feet high, and she would still be only 5' 1¾". I couldn't tell her that – the air was too thin and the oxygen was too valuable. The sun came up and Booker's tobacco-shrivelled lungs and oxygen-starved brain got him to the rim of the crater – Gilman's Point; no mean feat, almost due for his pension and reaching 18,630 feet.

I staggered onwards and upwards towards the summit, left far behind by the reindeer herders, the fake tan walkers and the Aussie butterfly twitcher. Only Cheffers plodded on behind me. How I struggled; the pain, the suffering and the drugs took their toll – I feel exhausted just thinking about it. Once at the top I felt like a short, fat, wheezing tub of lard in total meltdown. What is worse, so I was told, I looked like a short, fat, wheezing tub of lard in total meltdown – but not quite as bad as Cheffers. So the hours of training on my recently acquired waddling machine paid off, but I felt wrecked, physically and mentally.

It was my third time to the summit – *never, NEVER* again will I allow myself to be lured onto the slopes of Mount Kilimanjaro – beware of hat-tricks. The only other thing I have ever done twice is propose to be married – the replies were both in the negative – although the second negative followed a positive and a change of mind – at least that proves I proposed to a woman; I don't think I'll risk another hat-trick.

Going down – what a relief, but at 16,000 feet and climbing – a brilliant sulphur winged butterfly going up, where was it going? Would it go over the top? Would it get altitude sickness? Would it propose marriage? Do butterflies get married?

Booker was on the long dusty path downwards – his face wreathed in smiles. 'Page,' he said, as that is how ageing ex-public school boys speak, 'that was wonderful – that was Africa.' Oh dear – he was beginning to *Blixenate* again.

Monday September 30th

It was a wonderful feeling walking downhill. Tub of lard? I should think not – I am the conqueror of Africa's highest mountain – for the third time. Was I beginning to *Blixenate* too?

Good gracious; back at the national park entrance I was confronted by a most remarkable sight. Booker was taking huge bundles of money from each adventurer, including the now-recovered Nick and Dr Duncan. He was collecting it of course, not in Euros, nor sterling amazingly, but in US Dollars. He had turned himself into a type of Common Agricultural Policy, taking money from the rich to give to the poor – or rather more accurately – to the porters – helping to make the rich very short of cash. With flailing arms and wild, wide eyes and dishevelled hair, he gave a speech thanking them for their help and dishing out his subsidy. It was David Livingstone, meets *Out of Africa* meets Prof. C. J. Kilimanjaro Barkworth, meets Ken Dodd. He was *Blixenating* like I had never seen it before! In his case it was almost certainly genetic, caused by the blood pulsing vigorously through the Booker veins. In 1872 an ancestor – Bishop Coleridge Patteson, Bishop of Melanasia, was eaten by the natives – consumed by his congregation – I could see how and why it had happened.

At supper to celebrate I bought a bottle of wine to share with Sarah – it had a very attractive label. Ugh – it was Kenyan and even worse than before – a cocktail of alcoholic Windowlene and Harpic – we finished it up of course, to prevent dehydration.

OCTOBER

Tuesday October 1st

Somewhere, somehow Booker has found a telephone that works – don't tell Tilly and Alan what has hit the headlines in England – don't mention the reindeer. Oh dear, as we had been going up the mountain, with Alan and Tilly well in the lead, two ramblers in Scotland had been rapidly descending their particular mountain – courtesy of a rampant reindeer bull. For the first time in fifty years a rutting reindeer bull had taken great exception to ramblers close to his harem and he had tried to roll them down the mountain.

One brave woman defended her husband with a Thermos flask, finally pouring hot tea over the fiesty beasty. It obviously preferred coffee and fled, leaving the battered rambler to be flown off the hill by helicopter. Fortunately, by the

time Father Christmas arrives the reindeer rut will be over and in any case the bull reindeer concerned will have become a bullock. I expect by then Christopher Booker will be collecting money to buy our heroine a new Thermos flask.

Wednesday October 2nd

Tsavo West – in a valley of thorns, boulders and heat – a butterfly is travelling as fast as the Land Rover. Its wings are the colour of fake tan – it's a **monarch**. *IT IS A **MONARCH*** – it is the same **monarch** that sometimes arrives in Britain – can I count it? The answer seems to be *No*, I cannot. What a disappointment.

Friday October 4th

Palm trees, a warm breeze and the sound of surf as the Indian Ocean washes over white sand. It is wonderful lying by the pool after all our exertions. I feel tired – too tired to be decadent. What's that? Four wings – a bird that looks astonishingly like a pied wagtail is chasing a butterfly that looks astonishingly like a **monarch**. Bird and butterfly – butterfly and bird – circles – evasion and invasion – the

butterfly has got away. But was it a **monarch**? Things are never quite what they appear to be. Apparently, to a bird the **monarch** makes a rather unpleasant munch – not a lunch – once tasted, never again. As a caterpillar it eats various poisons in its diet which are retained in the body of both the caterpillar and the butterfly, as toxins – yes, a toxic, organic butterfly becomes unpalatable even poisonous to bird and beast. Not only does the **monarch** in Africa perform this indigestible trick – so does the **marbled white** in Britain.

But in Africa there are other edible butterflies who *mimic* the **monarch** – the female looks like a **monarch** – but she is not a **monarch** and does not taste like a **monarch**. So have I just seen a **monarch** – or a *mimic* **monarch** and does the wagtail know which is which – **monarch** or **African Queen** – they both sound very regal. Even more muddling – how does the **monarch** *mimic*, *mimic* the **monarch** in the first place? Yet it does so, by colour, by size and even by slower flight.

So from a butterfly comes another little message from nature – to all those who claim that organic food is non-chemical, clean and healthy, sorry – some organic plants produce wonderful toxins as good as any chemical spray. Anybody fancy some 'organic' deadly nightshade jam? It is strange too – I have never heard of anybody going in to my local doctor and saying, 'doctor, doctor, treat me I'm ill – but only give me organic drugs.' They are given synthesised chemicals in various forms – and nearly all the patients survive. So thank you butterflies – some females are not always what they appear to be and some natural food will fill you full of toxins far faster than eating junk burgers and chips.

Sunday October 6th

I woke up late. The sun was streaming though the window and there were no butterflies to be seen anywhere – just birds – birds with very short legs – house sparrows, chaffinches and a robin – I must be home.

A minor miracle has occurred. Somehow Colin the cucumber has not only hung on – he has flourished while I have been away. Sadly Colin has the wrong name – perhaps it should have been Colleen – as she, he or it has produced the smallest baby cucumber I have ever seen – half an inch long and perfectly formed. I picked it carefully and sent it to Sarah – her very own harvest – a cucette.

Monday October 7th

Sarah phoned. Can you believe it? She has not eaten the cucumber – she has fed it to her hamster – to Leroy. Oh dear – what gratitude.

Thursday October 10th

Tilly phoned – no butterflies but more trouble on the hill – someone else has been attacked. Yes Tilly, the reindeer herder, is also a wild boar keeper and she has been bowled over by a wild boar. As it rushed by, one of its razor sharp tusks slashed a wrist. Always prepared, Alan staunched the flow of blood, using a dirty piece of baler twine as a tourniquet. She was rushed off to Elgin hospital where she was stitched up and given a dose of penicillin. The notes from the non-organic medicine makers SmithKline Beecham Pharmaceuticals were very helpful: 'See your doctor immediately if you notice your urine become darker or your faeces (otherwise known as poo) becoming paler.' What was it Bomber Blair said again: 'Education, Edukation, Edukashun'?

Friday October 11th

The police phoned and left a message from Gloucestershire – they have had complaints – what I wonder? Shingles, diarrhoea or chicken pox? No, apparently, complaints about me.

Saturday October 19th

Exmoor – stopping off point on my way to Cornwall to talk about the farming crisis – could it be my lucky day – please let it be my **monarch** day. It is sunny but windy and the stag hounds are dropping down into a valley – no, the stag hounds do not touch the stag – that is known as misinformation – the stag stands at 'bay.' The icecream van is doing good trade – it follows the hunt throughout the winter – selling icecream on icy Exmoor in December and January. It means only two possibilities – either that the icecream of Exmoor is exceptionally good – or the people of Exmoor have no teeth.

There must have been two thousand people trying to follow the hunt by car. These were not people with plums in their mouths – or even damsons but rrrrr's. I have never hearrrrrrrd sentences and worrrrrrrds with so many

rrrrrr's in them. That will be the next ruling – New Labour in conjunction with the BBC, will ban all rrrrrrregional rrrrrrustic accents.

Suddenly – on a hilltop – at great speed – travelling with the wind comes – not a stag – not a hound – but a butterfly – coming, coming, gone. It was large and dark – not large and brown – almost certainly a *peacock*.

Sunday October 20th

The rain is raining – the wind is blowing when suddenly a large, brown flapping thing almost hit my windscreen. I screeched to a halt. Is it a *monarch*? – it's a fallen autumn oak leaf.

Thursday October 24th

As Eric swung into my sister Rachael's drive a new, bright, pristine *red admiral* settled on the gatepost. Eric stopped – almost without instruction – what a beautiful, perfect butterfly. How long will butterflies keep flying – when will my Safari be well and truly over? Will I see this *red admiral* again – in the spring?

Sunday October 27th

My late father's birthday – what gales. Trees have blown down – people have been killed – I have had to travel down to Brecon – Boyo – with Mick – to deliver copies of *The Feather and the Furrow* to a book warehouse. A falling branch nearly hit us and all the Herefordshire cider apples and perry pears have been picked by nature.

Monday October 28th

The calm after the storm and a strong new ***brimstone*** butterfly – in my garden – how did she survive the gale? Now she must find somewhere to hibernate – to survive the winter.

The cattle have not walked up to the farm today – so many berries have been blown off the hedgerows that they don't need hay or straw. They are eating the fallen hedgerow harvest. As soon as the weather changes and prolonged rain comes – I will have to put them in the yard for winter.

NOVEMBER

Sunday November 3rd

One last random effort to see a ***monarch***. One last journey to Norfolk – with Sarah at the wheel. We met Nigel and Barbara for an end of Safari pub lunch – Barbara still likes Nigel's pink socks. There are no bright colours anywhere else, only the changing browns and bronzes of autumn. There are no bright wings – only the wings of pigeons and peewits – in their winter flocks. The rams are in with the flocks of ewes – they have done their autumn task – they have no need to read that famous verse – poem – literary classic, of that fine countryman – Christopher Curtis.

> 'I'm a well-endowed ram and I got where I am
> By performing my act right on cue.
> When it's time for a tup, I just line 'em all up
> And shout 'volunteers?' Ewe, ewe and ewe!'

The season has changed and is changing – autumn has almost become winter.

Alas, we saw no ***monarch*** – it is still *fifty-eight* seen and I am rapidly running out of time.

Monday November 11th

How extraordinary – a Gloucestershire Police Sergeant telephoned again. He wants to take a statement from me about my speech at Frampton-on-Severn. That's fine – but why has it taken so long from September 8th to November 11th? He will come and see me next Monday. It is very odd – in the last two years my farm and that of Tim the tenant have been broken into or burgled eleven times and we can't get a policeman to visit. Now a Sergeant Clark wants to drive all the way from Gloucestershire to take a statement from me in Cambridgeshire – about what he would not say – he sounded rather evasive – or even embarrassed. Very peculiar – is it really the Gloucestershire Constabulary or the Blair Thought Police?

Friday November 15th

Oh no – an email from Cornwall – 'news of butterflies is getting sparse now but one record on the Migrant Moths website may be of interest – this is a sighting of a **monarch** butterfly at Hayle on the north Cornish coast on November 12th. Presumably it was a genuine transatlantic insect but as it was seen just outside a pub, there is I suppose some doubt about the observer's state of mind (very little doubt, I'm sure)'.

I decided not to leave for Cornwall on what was probably a wild, alcoholic butterfly chase.

Monday November 18th

What an extraordinary day. Two policemen turned up from Gloucestershire – not one – well one was a woman – and they didn't want a statement – they wanted an 'interview under caution'. As I had no solicitor with me – only Nigel – I refused. 'You're under arrest' said Sergeant Clark. Nigel went white: he trembled – he looked apopleptic – yes Nigel, this is Britain in the 21st Century – Britain under Blair – Britain eighteen years after George Orwell's Classic; for 1984 – read 2002; for the Thought Police read Gloucestershire Constabulary; for Big Brother read Tony Blair; for Air Strip One read Britain.

It is not funny hearing the cell door slam behind you. But suddenly there I was, unbelievably in the slammer at Parkside Police Station in Cambridge. One minute expecting a short conversation with a policeman – before returning to feed my cows – the next put into a police car and carted off to a cell – not bad for a current District Councillor.

The cell was not a pleasant place. There were dried faeces – sorry poo – on the wall – more dried faeces – sorry poo – and fag ends by the dirty toilet in the corner. In runnier, sunnier circumstances – ideal conditions for the **purple emperor**. I was glad I didn't need the loo.

My sports shoes were outside – laces were not allowed inside the cell in case I tried to harm myself. My badges were taken away too, in case I was tempted to stab myself with safety pins; 'Blair Britain's Mugabe' and 'Blair = B Liar' lay in a plastic bag together with my belt. Mobile phone, tape recorder, handkerchief

and all my money – tuppence. The Gloucestershire Constabulary had got their man.

Simply to get out I finally agreed to be interviewed under caution. Incredibly my crime was not searching for butterflies – but 'inciting racial hatred'. Good heavens – don't say a 'black, vegetarian, Muslim, asylum-seeking, one-legged lesbian lorry driver' had been in the audience at Frampton – and even if she had been – what on earth did I say to incite anything, apart from smiles and scepticism about the motives of this anti-countryside government?

Apparently somebody in Gloucestershire had complained – he had been 'upset' and on the random strength of that I had been arrested, although the unfortunate Sgt Clark could produce no evidence that I had broken any law. I was released on police bail to appear at Stroud police station in January – incredibly Air Strip One is obviously up and running. (As it turned out I was not required to go to Stroud – the police dropped their action – an action they should never have started in the first place. They almost certainly broke the law themselves by detaining me with absolutely no evidence of a crime having taken place.)

Home again – Sarah phoned: 'Any sign of a **monarch** yet?' she enquired. 'No,' I replied, 'all I have seen is the inside of a police cell.' She was flabbergasted: 'Do you mean that I have been on a Butterfly Safari with a crim?'

Strange to say my phone has behaved in a most extraordinary way this year. It has repeatedly gone dead and made strange noises. Engineers have gone up poles and down holes – but still my phone is the only one in the road to give trouble.

Then a new 'engineer' appeared. In exasperation I said: 'Tell me – is my phone being tapped?' To which I expected the reply 'Of course not, Sir'. The actual reply was: 'I'm sorry Sir, I can't answer that question as I'm bound by the Official Secrets Act'. Well, well, well – the tappers and buggers would have learnt a lot about butterflies during the course of the year.

Tuesday November 19th

The end of the butterfly season is the mirror image of the start. A **small tortoise-shell** is fluttering against the window pane of my study. I took it to the cool of the spare bedroom where it can sleep in peace until the spring. There will no 'hoovering' until April.

DECEMBER

Wednesday December 4th

I thought of *butterflies* today. How do they store enough food to get them through the winter? And what made me think of this? I travelled to Hereford to talk to the Hereford Agricultural Society. Nigel went with me to dish out CRT pamphlets. We arrived early and so went for a slap-up supper of fish and chips and mushy peas and then made our way to the Hereford Farmers Club.

How peculiar, we were ushered into the banqueting suite and tables were already laid for a meal – a slap-up Christmas dinner – I had forgotten. The day has certainly allowed me to store up fat for the winter.

Wednesday December 25th – Christmas Day

It is good to know that Tilly and Alan have had no more trouble with their reindeer as Father Christmas has left me a wonderful sparkly butterfly – a **swallowtail** – not sparkly pink, but sparkly silver. I will hang it from my living room light to remind me of its fifty-eight friends.

Tuesday December 31st

The last day of the year and what a year – one I will always remember. But as I look at my garden and the fields beyond, what am I seeing? Somewhere, somehow there are live butterflies out there, in hibernation – the **peacock**, the **small tortoiseshell**, the **brimstone**, the **comma** and, I believe one or two **red admirals**. But that is not all – there is the chrysalis (the pupa) of the **orange tip**, the **large white**, the **small white** and the **holly blue** – the caterpillar (the larva) of the **common blue**, the **brown argus** and I hope the **marbled white**. The **speckled wood** has to be different and can spend the winter either as a chrysalis or as a caterpillar. And that is not all – some butterflies, particularly some **hairstreaks** remain as eggs throughout the winter. I hope, unknown to me, still as eggs – there are some *white letter hairstreaks* in our remnant elms – next year when the sun is hot in high summer – I will search and hope to find.

The world of the butterfly is so fragile and delicate – so finely balanced – how does a butterfly's egg survive an English winter? How does it evade the eye of pheasant and blue tit and avoid flood, frost and plough? Butterfly lives are incredible lives – and my life seems fuller because I have found them and seen them.

But all is not well – thirty-five species of our resident butterflies are in decline through development, pollution and industrial farming. Yet, they are an indicator species – they indicate our care for their world – our world – and if they are in decline, our care is sadly lacking, our world is in decline. I believe that if we look after nature – nature will look after us: if we ignore nature, then nature will ignore us – and from the state of our butterflies we are ignoring nature. There is a threat to butterflies and so there is a threat to our world too.

I phoned Sarah to wish her a Happy New Year. She was still thinking of the old year: 'The Great British Butterfly Safari was wonderful Robin' she said, 'it's just a pity that none of the butterflies were pink.'

EPILOGUE

I CANNOT BELIEVE IT – I can really – when at secondary school my GCE marks in Maths were so low that I must have spelt my name wrong on the exam paper. I have counted the butterfly total again, and again, and again – the total is *fifty-nine* species seen not *fifty-eight*.

FIFTY-NINE

Even better than I had first thought – and what butterfly did I miss out of the count? The **small heath**. What an insult to a small but important little butterfly. So – I apologise – profusely and abjectly to the **small heath**.

It also means that all those kind people who sponsored me – butterfly by butterfly – were undercharged by one butterfly.

Never mind – so far over £11,000 has been raised for The Gordon Beningfield Memorial Appeal by butterfly sponsorship. The Appeal – run by The Countryside Restoration Trust – to buy a farm in Dorset as a living tribute to the life and work of Gordon Beningfield. If you have enjoyed this book and wish to contribute, donations please to the The Countryside Restoration Trust, Barton, Cambs CB3 7AG.

The Countryside Restoration Trust – Gordon was a Founder Trustee of the CRT. The Trust is a registered charity and is dedicated to farming and wildlife in the general countryside. The aim is the production of quality food, while attracting and encouraging wildlife and at the same time creating proper jobs for a living, working countryside. Details again from The Countryside Restoration Trust, Barton, Cambs CB3 7AG.

Butterfly Conservation – Gordon Beningfield was a patron and a keen supporter of Butterfly Conservation – the charity specialising in butterflies and moths. B.C. gave me considerable help during the entire Great British Butterfly

Safari and without their help the final number of species seen would certainly not have been *fifty-nine*. Details of Butterfly Conservation from – Butterfly Conservation, Manor Yard, East Lulworth, Wareham, Dorset BH20 5QP.

The Field Studies Council – the producer of the excellent butterfly chart, is an independent educational charity bringing environmental understanding to all, through courses, training and publications. The Field Studies Council, Preston Montford, Shrewsbury SY4 1HW.

Bird's Farm Books – my own little back-room publishing company – created to both promote and defend the traditional countryside. For details of books past, present and future write to Bird's Farm Books, Barton, Cambs CB3 7AG.

There are many people to thank for making the Great British Butterfly Safari such a success. First and foremost I must thank Sarah Golding for being so positive and happy during what were some very long, gruelling days and weeks of butterfly-hunting. Sarah's ugly stand-ins Tim Scott, Mick Brown and Nigel Housden were all vital in verifying some of the butterflies – and were, for good measure, good company.

Martin Warren of Butterfly Conservation, Matthew Oates of the National Trust, Simon Spencer and Val Perrin were all important in allowing me to reach the final total. Others who gave me much butterfly help were Miriam Rothschild, David Redhead, Trevor Grange, John Wilson, Tony Tutton, Greg Herbert, John Halliday, Malcolm Read, Peter Moule, Simon Elliot and John and Ena Hume. David and Ingrid Grayling were also very helpful in the Lake District. Thanks are also due to Rebecca Farley and the Field Studies Council for permission to include their beautiful chart – Guide to the Butterflies of Britain – with *The Great British Butterfly Safari*.

Others helped me by looking after the farm, the CRT and Bird's Farm Books while I was chasing butterflies particularly Rachael Page, John Page, and Mary and Brian West. Mick Brown, Nigel Housden and Tim Scott were again vital in keeping things running at home. I am sure I have forgotten someone in the rush to get the book out – sorry. I have made every effort to obtain permission to quote poetry. Where I have failed to find the source, I apologise.

Finally, a thank you to Christopher Booker for all his encouragement and support of the Safari; to Willie Poole for his Foreword; to John Paley for his magnificent cartoons; to Margaret for her frantic rushing about to get the book out and to Jim and Franca at Book Production Consultants who put the whole thing together with the minimum of tears.

There must also be a thank you to the butterflies themselves which were wonderful – who knows? – I expect I will soon be talking to them on a regular basis

Safari Who's Who

Ken Livingstone – the first elected Mayor of London – because his publicity machine tells people he has newts as pets – it is assumed by some, quite wrongly, that he is an expert on wildlife and conservation – yes, Ken – thank you Ken – that green thing with leaves and a trunk – we call a tree.

John Prescott MP – once a working-class old-Labour firebrand who went on strike. Now a New Labour non-lover of strikers and lover of large cars – yes, John – thank you John – they are terraced houses we are passing where Labour voters live.

Tony Blair MP – an ex-public school Oxford graduate of the type normally associated with the Tory Party. He is Leader of the Labour Party and Prime Minister. His ambition seems to be that he wants to become the President of Europe or even King of the World – although some of his wicked detractors cruelly say that his body language suggests he would rather be Queen – yes, Tone – thank you Tone – one is a bomb and one is a testosterone tablet – which one would you prefer at your time of life?

Bomber Blair MP – *see above.*

Cherie Blair – not an MP – the lovely, pouting wife of the Prime Minister. She comes from a poor background, so it is said, and has overcome adversity to become Mrs Blair. She now wants to become a Judge – yes, Cherie – thank you Cherie – he is a criminal and he can arrange a good discount for you if you want to buy a couple of flats in Bristol.

Stephen Byers MP – a little-known New Labour Member of Parliament who became a Minister under the patronage of Bomber Blair. After wicked and dishonest accusations against him of sleaze, lies and lie-ins he tragically resigned. I am afraid I can remember nothing more about him – yes, Stephen – thank you Stephen – yes, I'm sure you were very famous once.

Christopher Booker – a man – but almost a saint. A seeker after truth and a scourge of all evil empires and empire builders – the EU, the EU, the EU and finally the EU. One of his missionary ancestors was murdered by natives – I prefer the version that had him eaten from the pot – yes, Christopher – thank you Christopher – that is an OBE, that is an MBE, that is a Knighthood and that is a Peerage – all things that you will never get.

Ken Dodd – a rare comedian these days, who decided to ply his trade on the stage and not in the House of Commons.

Joanna Lumley – a live celebrity, very popular with other live celebrities.

Spike Milligan – a deceased celebrity, still very popular with live middle-aged and elderly celebrities.

Alun Michael MP – hallo … hallo … HALLOOO … anybody there?

Sir James Goldsmith – a brave and enlightened man who fought to save the endangered pound, through keeping Britain a free and independent country. As a lover of freedom, and as a do-it-yourself politician, he faced much opposition – particularly from politicians of the politically correct variety.

John Aspinall – a brave and enlightened man who fought to save endangered wildlife through captive breeding in his wonderful zoos, in the hope that one day they could be given back their freedom with security. As a conservationist he faced much opposition, especially from conservationists of the politically correct variety.

BBC – the Brussels Broadcasting Corporation – the BBC once the face of public service broadcasting – now the face of the politically correct establishment. Free speech abroad is championed. Free speech at home, which criticises the BBC, is branded as 'trouble making'.

BBC2 – the Blair Broadcasting Corporation – a subsidiary of the Brussels Broadcasting Corporation – used by the politically correct, or so it seems to many, as a weapon of mass deception.